Other Regal Venture Books by Ethel Barrett
The Strangest Thing Happened...
Which Way to Nineveh?
The People Who Couldn't Be Stopped
The Secret Sign
I'm No Hero
Rules, Who Needs Them?
If I Had a Wish
God and a Boy Named Joe
God, Have You Got It All Together?

These Regal Venture books make Bible stories come alive for readers of every age. They also provide exciting resources for G/L pre-teens Bible studies.

ETHEL BARRETT
tells Bible Stories to children
Volume 2

A Division of G/L Publications
Glendale, California, U.S.A.

© Copyright 1977 by G/L Publications
All rights reserved.

Published by
Regal Books Division, G/L Publications
Glendale, California, 91209

Printed in U.S.A.
Library of Congress Catalog Card No. 76-45256
ISBN 0-8307-0475-2

Contents

Ways to Use This Book **7**

PART 1   STORIES OF MOSES
Story 1   A Secret in a Basket **12**
Story 2   A Surprise for a Princess **17**
Story 3   The Boy Who Became a Prince **21**
Story 4   The Burning Bush That Didn't Burn **25**
Story 5   The Journey That Began at Midnight **30**
Story 6   The People Who Couldn't Go Backwards **34**
Story 7   The Grumble-Mumble People **38**
Story 8   Too Many Gifts **43**
Story 9   The Wonderful Church in the Wilderness **47**
Story 10   Stop, Look and Listen **51**
Story 11   Two Against Ten **55**
Story 12   More Grumble-Mumbles **60**
Story 13   The Laws That Lasted Forever **65**
SONG   Psalm 86:5 **69**

PART 2	STORIES OF JESUS
Story 14	The Greatest Promise in the World **72**
Story 15	The Promise Comes True **76**
Story 16	The Strangest Announcement in the World **80**
Story 17	Two Dreams That Saved a Little Child **84**
Story 18	When Jesus Was a Little Boy **89**
Story 19	When Jesus Was a Big Boy **93**
Story 20	Lost: One Boy **97**
Story 21	The Children Find a Friend **101**
Story 22	The Boy the Doctors Couldn't Cure **105**
Story 23	The Man Who Couldn't See **109**
Story 24	The Most Extraordinary Lunch in the World **114**
Story 25	The Man Who Went Through the Roof **118**
Story 26	The Day Jesus Didn't Hurry **122**
Story 27	An Exciting Day in Jerusalem *(Palm Sunday)* **126**
Story 28	The Saddest Day *(Good Friday)* **130**
Story 29	The Gladdest Day *(Easter)* **134**
Story 30	The Best News! (Ascension) **139**
SONG	Jesus Loves Me, Jesus Loves Me **143**

When you see one of these (*) look at the bottom of the page.

WAYS TO USE THIS BOOK

"Read some more!" is one of the most rewarding compliments a listener can give, for it reflects his feelings of wanting to repeat a pleasant experience.

WHY READ TO A CHILD?

Listening to a good story, well read, has many values for a child. It helps him learn to listen and thus increases his attention span. Listening to a good story also helps him develop his ability to retain a sequence of ideas. As he talks with you about a story he has heard, he gains experience in speaking and thus increases his vocabulary. And when your child snuggles down beside you to hear a story, an emotional closeness develops from this warm and personal interaction.

WHY READ BIBLE STORIES?

Our purpose in reading Bible stories to a child is to share with him the gospel of God's love and the meaning of that love for everyone. It's also a way of telling him WE highly value what God says to us in the Bible.

Reading and talking about Bible stories provide natural value-teaching situations. For example, in Story 12, Moses disobeys God by striking the rock. This story offers a natural opportunity to talk about the unhappiness disobedience brings.

STORY READING TIPS

1. Read daily. The length of time isn't as important as its regularity. Some parents make story reading a bedtime ritual. Others include story time as a part of family times.

2. Read expressively. Let your voice reflect your enthusiasm for what you're reading so that your genuine interest in the story comes through. Add "sound effects" to the words you read. For example, " 'Why did you bring us here?' they asked Moses. Mumble-grumble-mumble. 'Why didn't you leave us in Egypt?' Mumble-grumble. 'There is no fruit.' Grumble-mumble . . . . 'And now there isn't even any WATER!' Mumble-GRUMBLE."

Create excitement by speaking slightly faster. Whisper or pause briefly to add suspense. For example, " 'It's the rumble of chariot wheels!' And the people scrambled out of their tents to listen. The rumble grew louder. . . . 'It IS Pharaoh!' They shouted. 'And all his soldiers! They're coming after us!' "

Change the tone of your voice to identify and reflect the feelings of the Bible story characters. For instance, " 'Your son did not die!' they cried. " 'He is well!' "

" 'I know—I know!' said the nobleman. 'Jesus healed him!' And they all started back for the house.

" 'Just when,' asked the nobleman, 'did my son start to get better?' "

" 'About one o'clock,' they cried. 'Yes—it was just one o'clock.' "

" 'Ahhh,' he said quietly . . . 'For that is just the hour Jesus said to me, 'Go back home—your son is well.' "

3. Read creatively. Young children, particularly, thrive on repetition. After your child has become familiar with a story, omit a word and let him "fill in the blank." Of course, the word should be an important one, such as an action word or a person's name.

4. Follow the story with fun-to-do activities. Include the "Let's Talk About the Bible Story" section (following each story) to help clarify ideas presented in the story; to discuss how story characters may have felt, and to think of how we might have felt in a similar situation. Take turns answering the questions to avoid a "test" atmosphere. Or, let each listener ask another family member one question about the story.

Provide appropriate art materials for your child to use in drawing or painting a picture of his favorite part of the story.

Help your child learn to repeat with understanding the Bible verse given at the conclusion of the "Let's Talk About" section. Talk together about the meaning of the verse. Ask, "What is another way to say this verse? . . ." Let him underline with a red pencil the verse in the Bible (to help him locate it easily).

A child who is learning to use his Bible will be interested in finding the story for himself. Guide him in locating the story in relation to the Old and New Testaments; also in relation to adjacent books in the Bible.

Sing together the songs included in this book (see "Contents") as a part of your fun-to-do activities.

PART ONE
STORIES OF MOSES

STORY 1

A SECRET IN A BASKET

Becky can't play this afternoon. She's stuck with her baby brother. She has to watch him while her mother gets some important things done in the house. How do you think Becky feels about it? Well, if you want to know the truth, she doesn't feel "stuck" at all. Actually she has a sneaky feeling of joy. It's really fun to take care of a baby. And it's WONDERFUL to be trusted with one!

Most big brothers and sisters help take care of the baby in the house or on the porch or in the yard. Can you imagine taking care of your baby brother while he's sleeping—in the RIVER? That happened once, to a big sister named Miriam. She took care of her baby brother, and it was no easy job. Because she lived long long ago—not in ORDINARY times. She lived in a time of TROUBLE.

The trouble all began with a wicked king called Pharaoh.

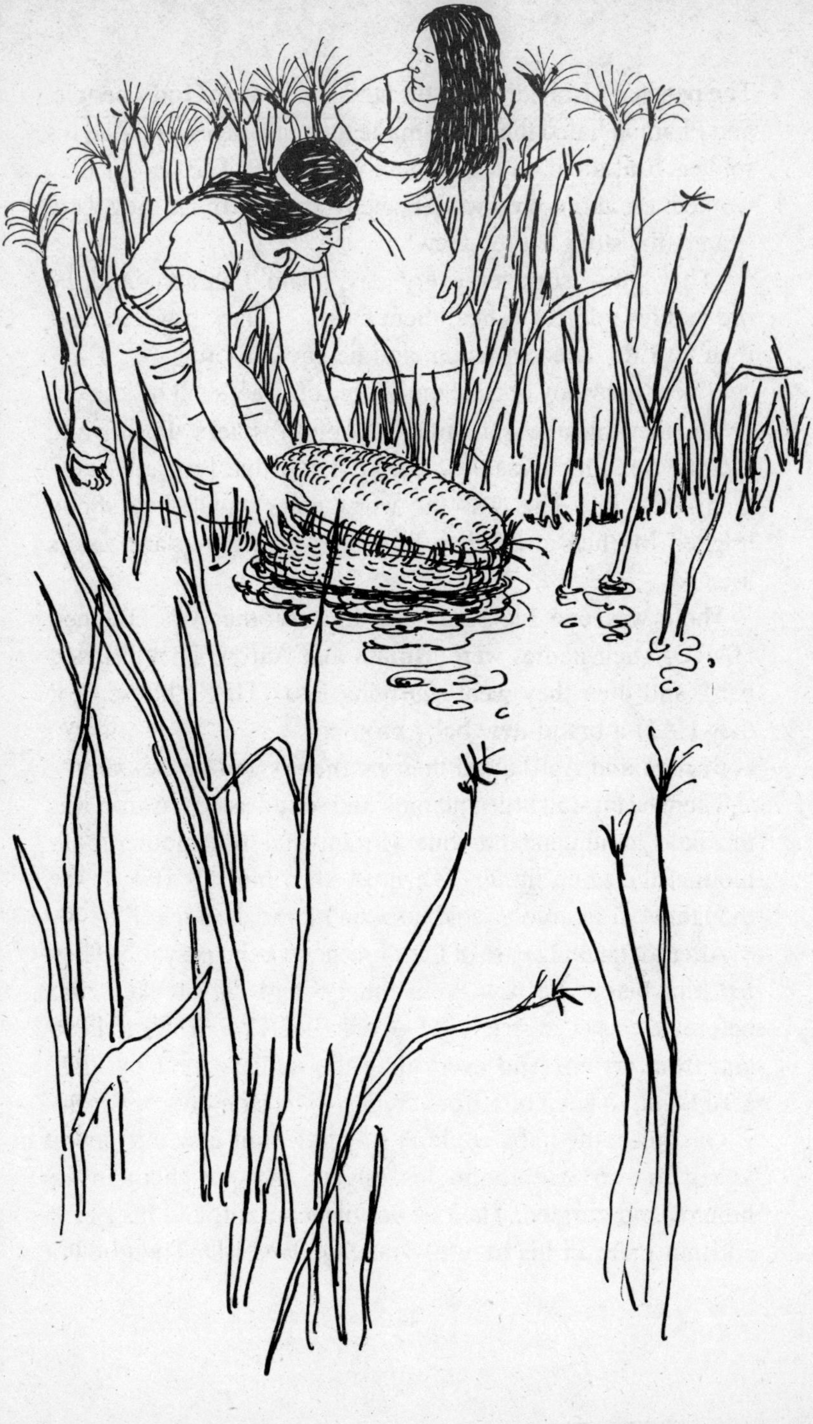

The people of Israel lived in his land. They were God's people, and Pharaoh hated them. He made them all slaves, and had his soldiers beat them, to make them work hard. The harder they worked, the more they were beaten—and the more they were beaten, the stonger they grew!

"They grow stronger every day," said Pharaoh, and he ordered his soldiers to beat them harder. "They grow stronger than EVER," cried Pharaoh, and he gave an order—

"Every baby boy born to the people of Israel shall be killed!"

What terrible news! It sent the people of Israel scurrying into their houses. Of course they already knew that Pharaoh hated them—but this! This was the worst news of all. Everybody listened. Mothers and fathers listened. And brothers and sisters listened.

There was one big sister and little brother who listened HARD. Their names were Miriam and Aaron. They listened hard, and then they went scurrying into THEIR house. For they HAD a brand-new baby brother!

Miriam and Aaron and their mother looked at the baby.

There he lay—all little and pink and sound asleep. Aaron was too little to understand—but Miriam and her mother both thought the same thing. "We must keep him QUIET," they thought—"so Pharaoh's soldiers won't know he's here!"

After that, taking care of their brother was no easy job. They fed him before he was even hungry—and they rocked him before he was even sleepy. They did EVERYTHING to keep him from crying. And every time the soldiers went by, they asked God to keep him from crying, so he wouldn't be found.

Of course, the baby couldn't stay little and pink and sound asleep forever. He found his fingers and put them in his mouth—and gurgled. Then he got bigger and found his FEET and put them in his mouth—and SQUEALED. Then he got bigger, and kicked his blankets off—and LAUGHED! Something had to be done!

Miriam knew her mother would think of SOMETHING. But what her mother thought of sent little prickles of fear right down Miriam's back! For this is what her mother did. She took some reeds, and wove a little basket, just like a cradle. She filled up the cracks with tar. "So it won't leak," she said.

"Leak?" said Miriam. "Where are you going to PUT him?"

"In the river," said her mother, and the prickles of fear came back again, up and down Miriam's back.

And sure enough—that's just what they did. Early the next morning they put baby Moses in the basket—and asked God to take care of him. Then they went down to the river and the mother waded out and tucked that little basket in among the tall grasses, called bulrushes, that were growing up out of the water.

"You stay close by," whispered Miriam's mother, "and watch him from the shore." And then she was gone.

Miriam watched and waited. She waited while the prickles of fear went up and down her back. She waited until—

VOICES!

Miriam held her breath. Were they soldiers? No—they were WOMEN'S voices! "Dear God," prayed Miriam, "take care of my baby brother, no matter WHAT happens!"

Miriam didn't know what WOULD happen, because the order from the king had been, "Every baby boy shall be killed!"

But she DID know that GOD was watching over that baby and that HE would keep him safe.

LET'S TALK ABOUT THE BIBLE STORY

Miriam didn't know what was going to happen, but she

trusted someone. Whom? That was a long time ago. Do you think we can trust the same One today? What are some times you didn't know what was going to happen, but you trusted God to help you?

A BIBLE VERSE TO LEARN

Cast all your anxiety on him because he cares for you. (1 Pet. 5:7, *NIV*)

LET'S TALK TO GOD

Dear God, we thank you that you still take care of us today the same way you took care of your children back in Bible times. Help us to trust you no matter WHAT happens. In Jesus' name, Amen.

NOW FIND THIS STORY IN YOUR BIBLE

It's in Exodus 1:8-22 and 2:1-4.

STORY 2

A SURPRISE FOR A PRINCESS

It certainly looked as if baby Moses didn't have a chance. There he was, rocking back and forth in a basket in the river. And there was his big sister Miriam watching from the shore. SHE couldn't help him. But God could!

When Miriam heard the women's voices, she crept through the reeds to peek—and stopped in her tracks. "It's the PRINCESS!" she gasped. "She's coming to bathe in the river!"

Sure enough, it was! Her beautiful dress was purple and gold. Her rings and bracelets glittered in the sunlight. Her maidens fanned her with large fans. She was a princess all right—and her father was THE WICKED PHARAOH!

Miriam looked back at the basket. It was rocking back and forth—"Oh dear," thought Miriam. "Is he awake? Is he KICKING? Oh DEAR!" And she thought, "Baby, be quiet—PLEASE be quiet!" And then—

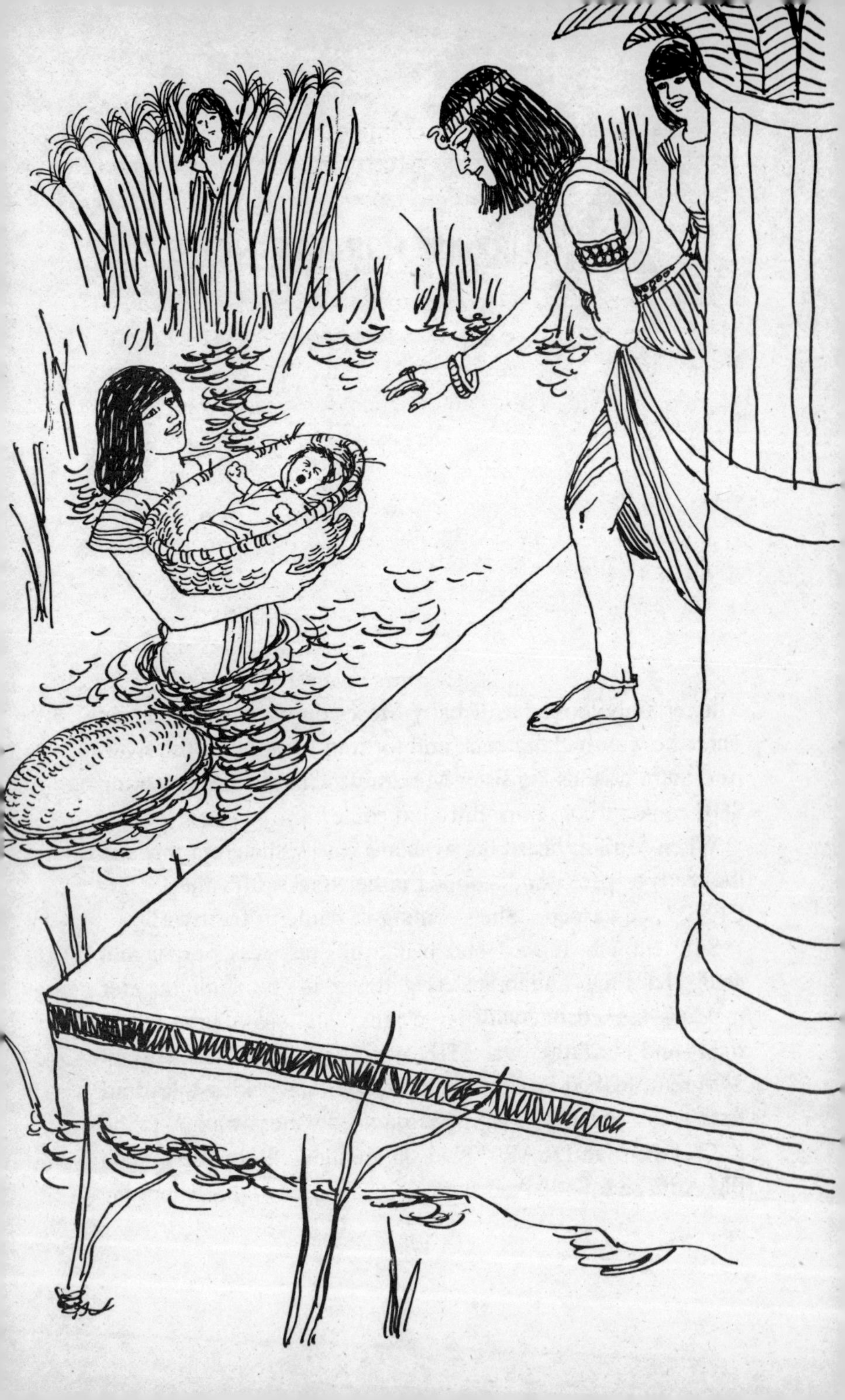

"What is that, floating over there?" It was the princess speaking. She has seen the basket! Miriam's heart almost stopped beating. She stumbled closer, and listened while the princess asked one of her maidens to bring the basket to her. She watched while the maiden waded over and got the basket. She held her breath while the princess and her maidens looked inside. The baby kicked his little feet. He doubled up his little fists. He puckered up his little face. And he cried! Oh, he cried HARD! Miriam almost fell over her own feet, to get closer.

"It's one of the Hebrew babies—it belongs to one of the people of Israel," said the princess, as she picked him up. "He's a beautiful baby," she crooned, as she held him close.

The maidens stood around, all excited. "What are you going to DO with him?" they asked.

The princess looked at the baby. The baby stopped crying for a minute, and looked at the princess. And then—

"I—I'm going to keep him," she said. "I'm going to call him Moses." Baby Moses began to cry again, as if this wasn't good news at all. But Miriam knew it was the best news in the world!

"You'll have to find him a nurse," said the maidens. And Miriam stumbled out of the reeds before she had time to even be frightened. She bowed to the princess—and her legs got all tangled up like a pretzel, she was so excited.

"Oh, princess!" she cried. "I know where you can get him a nurse!" And the princess looked at Miriam for a moment, and said—"All right. Go get me a nurse."

Miriam ran back to her mother so fast she could hardly get her breath, to tell her mother the wonderful news. And Miriam and her mother hurried back down to the river so fast—so fast! And at last they stood trembling before the princess.

"Take care of this baby for me," said the princess. "And I will pay you well." And she put baby Moses right where he belonged—right back in his mother's arms! Moses stopped crying, just as if he knew everything was going to be all right. And everything WAS all right! Moses snuggled up in his mother's arms—safe from the wicked Pharaoh's soldiers. Miriam and her mother had their baby back again, and the soldiers couldn't kill him now. He belonged to Pharaoh's daughter—the princess!

Yes, for awhile it had certainly looked as if baby Moses was in trouble. But God was watching out for him—and there were exciting things ahead!

LET'S TALK ABOUT THE BIBLE STORY

Miriam and her mother had to give baby Moses away for his own good. Have you ever had to part with something when it really HURT? (No—not a tooth; don't be smart.) Miriam certainly got the job done, didn't she? In order to get a job done you have to be in the right place at the right time. Can you think of times when you got a job done because you obeyed? Or times when jobs didn't get done because you disobeyed?

A BIBLE VERSE TO LEARN

Serve the LORD with all your heart. (1 Samuel 12:20, *KJV*)

LET'S TALK TO GOD

Dear God, help us to remember that when we obey, we're in the RIGHT place at the RIGHT time. Thank you for doing everything for our own good, even if it means that sometimes we have to give up something. In Jesus' name, Amen

NOW FIND THIS STORY IN YOUR BIBLE

It's in Exodus 2:5-10.

STORY 3

THE BOY WHO BECAME A PRINCE

Baby Moses belonged to the Pharaoh's daughter—a real live princess! And he had for a nurse—his own mother! And he lived—in his own house! How happy everybody was! Now Moses could kick and cry all he wanted to, and nobody cared. Miriam took him out in the sun and played with him—and nobody bothered them. It was wonderful. Oh joy!

But now they had to get busy. They had to teach him about God. They had to teach him to pray. So while he was still kicking in his basket, they crooned songs about God to him. While he was creeping around the house, they taught him to obey. And while he was learning to walk, they told him stories about God. And before you could say "Moses-in-the-bulrushes"—he had grown to be a little boy. And it was time for

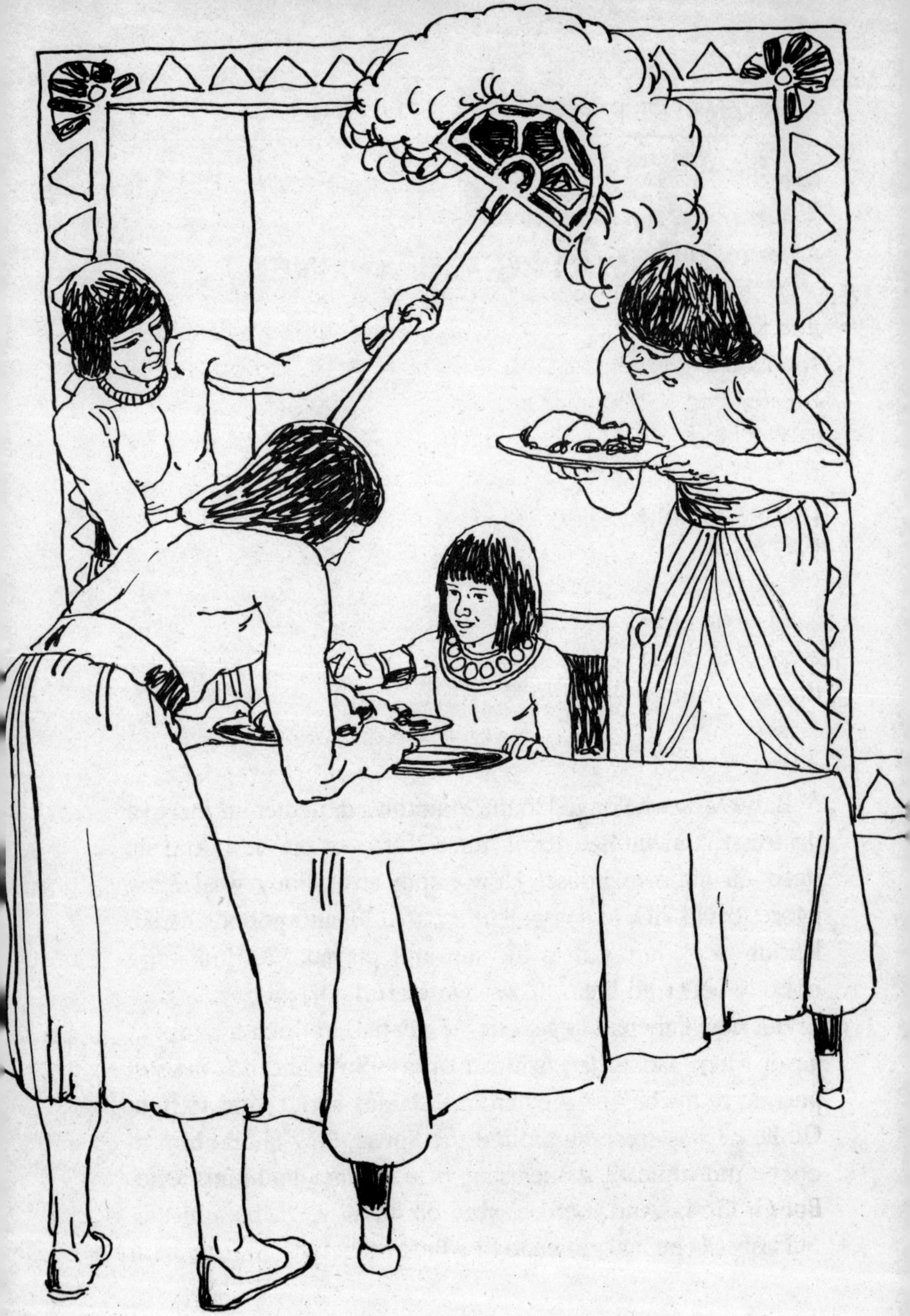

him to go to the palace and live with the princess.

How Moses' family hated to see him go! How hard it was to say good-by! As his mother left him with the princess, she remembered that God had spared his life—and she asked God to keep right on watching over him.

Moses looked at his new mother, with her beautiful gown and jewels. He looked at the shiny palace floors, and the huge rooms and the lovely gardens. And he took a deep, DEEP breath—and started his new life.

The fun was different. Instead of going for hikes, he went for rides in big chariots drawn by beautiful horses. Instead of playing in the streets with Miriam watching over him, he played in the palace gardens, with wonderful toys—and GUARDS watching over him.

The eating was different. Instead of helping to set the table, and going out to carry water—he had servants to bring him his dinner and his snacks on gold plates.

And the learning was different. Instead of listening to his mother, he had special teachers to come and help him learn to read and sing and do numbers and draw pictures. And there in the big palace, with all the soldiers and teachers and big marble statues and shiny floors—Moses learned to be a prince. And the princess and the teachers just PACKED his head full of learning.

But along with all the other things he was learning, Moses never forgot the things his real mother had taught him. He never forgot the songs. Or the stories about God. Or how to pray. And every night, before he went to bed, he prayed to God.

The princess and the teachers were watching over his head. But GOD was watching over his HEART!

The princess and the teachers were teaching him to be a

good prince. But GOD was teaching him to be a good LEADER. And in our next story—he IS!

LET'S TALK ABOUT THE BIBLE STORY

Did you ever try to pour water in a barrel that had a hole in the bottom? Well you don't have to—you KNOW what will happen. Sometimes instructions are like that—they go right out of your head as if you had a hole in it. God is trying to make something special out of Moses. What? How can Moses help? Are you supposed to pay attention to God's instructions just at home and in Sunday School? Where else should you pay attention to God's instructions?

A BIBLE VERSE TO LEARN

Remember also your Creator (that means God—and that means God's instructions) *in the days of your youth.* (Ecclesiastes 12:1, *NASB*)

LET'S TALK TO GOD

Dear God, sometimes it's awfully hard to go away from those we love. Especially when our heads are chock-full of "dos and don'ts" from everybody. We thank you that we can trust you to help us no matter WHERE we are or how strange it is. That's a good thing to know, God. We are very grateful. In Jesus' name, Amen.

NOW FIND THIS STORY IN YOUR BIBLE

It's in Exodus 2:8-10 and Acts 7:20-22.

STORY 4

THE BURNING BUSH THAT DIDN'T BURN

Now anybody knows that if you run away from something very frightening, the last thing in the world you'd want to do would be to go back to it. It would be like running away from a roaring lion—and having somebody ask you to go back and feed him your popcorn! And yet—that's what happened to Moses.

When Moses got to be a man, even though he was the son of the princess, he still loved the Hebrews, for they were his own people. And day after day, he saw them beaten and worked to death by the cruel Pharaoh's soldiers.

One day Moses tried to help one of these poor Hebrew men who was being beaten. Imagine the son of the PRINCESS helping a Hebrew SLAVE! It made the cruel Pharaoh so angry, that he was WORSE than a roaring lion—and Moses knew he would have to run away, or the Pharaoh would have him killed.

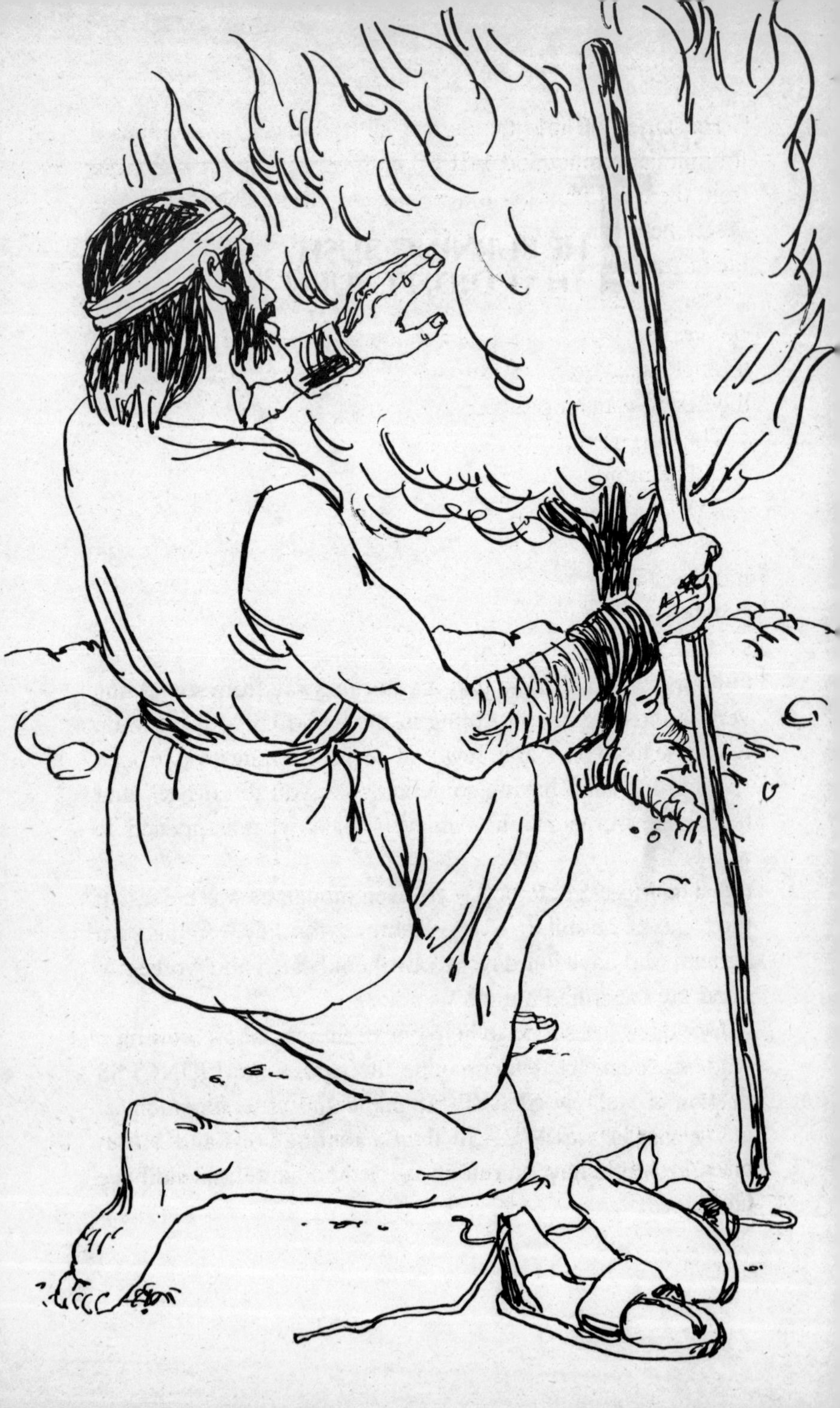

He started off into the desert—all by himself—and traveled for miles and miles and MILES until he was far enough away from the cruel Pharaoh to feel safe. And there, way off in the desert, he met a shepherd family and settled down to live with them. And there, he began a brand-new life.

How different it was! Instead of wearing beautiful princely clothes, he wore shepherd's clothes. Instead of wandering through palace gardens, he wandered along the grassy parts of the desert, watching sheep.

The days went by.

   The months went by.

      The YEARS went by.

And Moses felt less and less like a prince—and more and more like a shepherd. As he watched his sheep under the desert sun, he thought about his own people and his old home. As he sat under the stars at night, he thought about his real mother, and remembered the stories she had told him about God.

And then it happened. The most wonderful—and the most FRIGHTENING thing!

Moses was wandering along the desert with his sheep, when he saw it. It was a bush on fire. Now there was nothing so unusual about that—except that THIS bush was all on fire, but the leaves didn't curl up and fall off—and the branches didn't turn to ashes and drop. Right in the middle of all the fire, the leaves and branches stayed green and pretty and didn't seem to mind the fire a bit!

Moses just stood and stared. And then he heard a voice.

"Moses, Moses!" It was coming from the bush!

"Here I am," said Moses, and he stared some more.

"Take off your sandals," said the voice. "For this is a holy place." And then Moses knew. He took off his sandals. It was God!

"I know how cruel Pharaoh is to the Hebrew people," said God's voice. "I want you to go back and ask Pharaoh to let them go. I want you to be their leader, and lead them out of Egypt."

Why, that was worse than facing a lion! "I—I CAN'T," said Moses. "I can't do this great thing alone!"

And the voice said, "You won't HAVE to do it alone. Certainly I will be with you!"

And then the fire was gone. The bush was still there, but the fire was gone. And Moses was alone. He was afraid and excited, all at the same time. He knew he had a great and FRIGHTENING job to do. But he knew that God would be with him!

Once you've run away from something, the hardest thing in the world to do—is to go back. But there isn't ANYTHING you can't do—if God is with you.

LET'S TALK ABOUT THE BIBLE STORY

Can you think of times when you've run away from something very unpleasant, and then had to go back and face it? Can you think of times when someone has asked you to do something you thought you weren't able to do? What did you do about it? Did you remember that God was with you?

A BIBLE VERSE TO LEARN

God said, *"Certainly I will be with you."* (Exodus 3:12, *NASB*)

LET'S TALK TO GOD

Dear God, help us to remember that you are ALWAYS with us—in the good safe places and in the scary places. And when we're not able to do something by ourselves, we can always count on you. Help us always to be ready to do what you tell us to do. In Jesus' name, Amen.

NOW FIND THIS STORY IN YOUR BIBLE

It's in Exodus 2:11-25 and 3:1-12 and 4:1-17.

STORY 5

THE JOURNEY THAT BEGAN AT MIDNIGHT

Moses had a wonderful and FRIGHTENING job to do. But he knew he could do anything, because God was with him. And so he started back to Egypt to ask Pharaoh to let the Hebrew people go.

When Moses marched up to Pharaoh and said, "God says you must let the Hebrew people go!"—Pharaoh was FURIOUS.

"Who is God," he said, "that he should tell me what to do?"

But God punished Pharaoh, and Pharaoh changed his mind. And when Pharaoh cried, "All right! Let them go!"—it looked as if the job was DONE right then and there. But it wasn't.

The minute Pharaoh forgot his punishment, he changed his mind. "No," he cried, "they cannot go!"

So the job got harder.

God punished Pharaoh again, until he cried, "All right. Let them go!"

But as soon as they were ready to go—he changed his mind again!

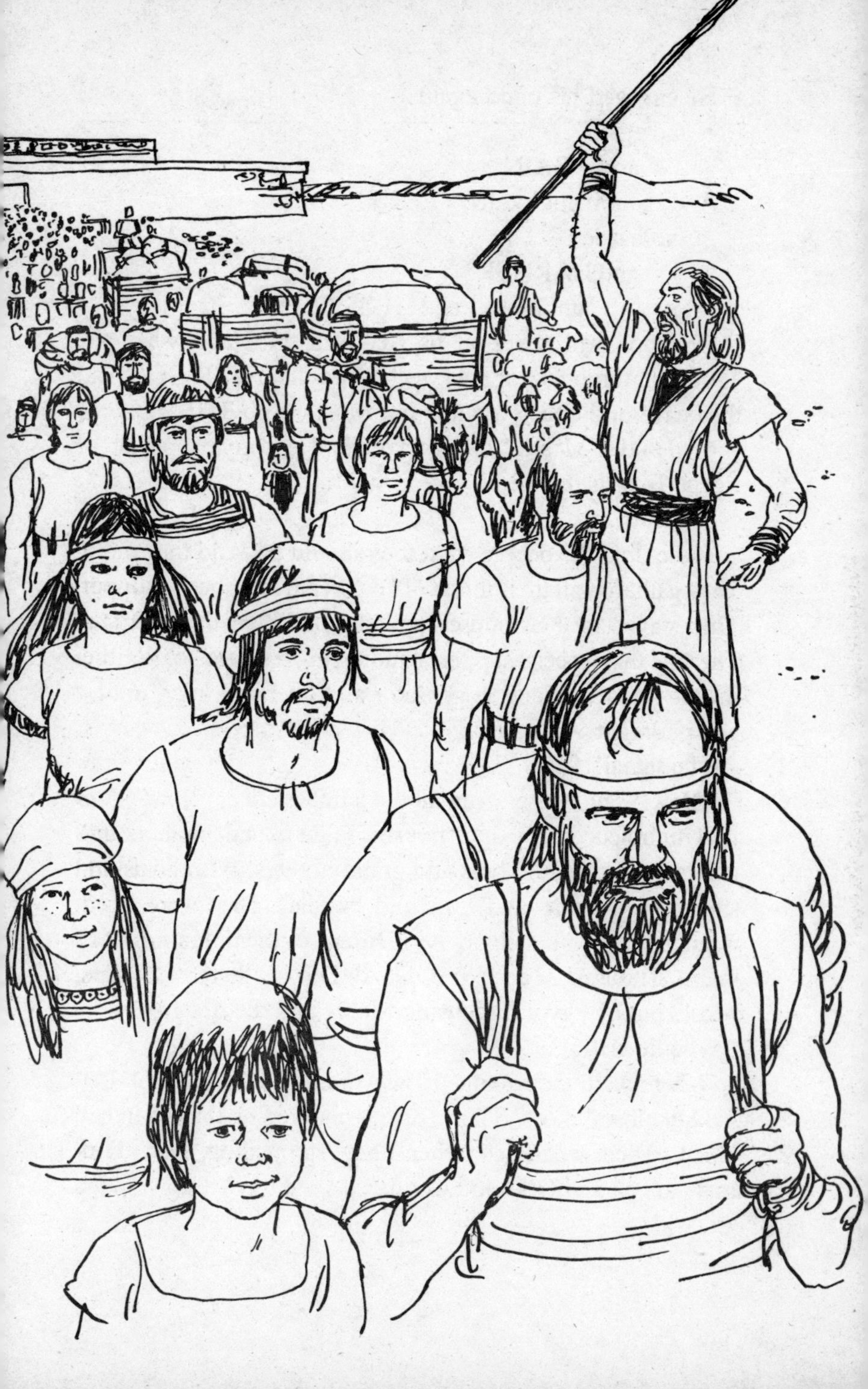

He changed his mind again
   and again
      and AGAIN.
And the job got harder
   and harder
      and HARDER
         until it looked IMPOSSIBLE.

"Pharaoh will never let us go," said the Hebrew people. "Today or tomorrow or next week. We will NEVER GO." And they gave up hope—everyone but Moses. And THEN—

God said to Moses, "Tonight you shall lead my people out of Egypt. Now is the time."

Tonight!

Moses told the people what they should do. And they did it. They gathered all their things. They prepared a special supper. They stayed in their houses—quietly—and waited. It got late. They ate their special supper, standing up, ready to go. Waiting for the signal. Quietly. It got later and later and later, until it was midnight. And then—

The signal!

"Now!" said Moses. And all the families cried, "Now!" And they tumbled out of their houses. Fathers and mothers and children and grandfathers and grandmothers. With goats and sheep and wagons and carts and bundles. They were like a mighty army, following Moses. Dozens of them. Hundreds of them. Thousands and THOUSANDS of them, following Moses out of Egypt. Following Moses into the desert—

The desert!

Where were they going? How would they know?

Did Moses know? The people wondered as they marched along. They wondered when they stopped to rest. They marched on and ON—and wondered. And then—they stopped in their tracks. There ahead of them was a great big cloud. Not like any other cloud they had ever seen. "It's God," they cried. "It's God, showing us which way to go!"

And it was!

The people followed the cloud all day. And at night when they couldn't see it—but they COULD see it. Because it changed into a pillar of fire!

And they marched on, free at last. They knew God was with them day and night. For they had a pillar of cloud by day and a pillar of fire by night to prove it to them!

LET'S TALK ABOUT THE BIBLE STORY

Of course God doesn't lead us with clouds and pillars of fire today—but He DOES lead us. Can you think of any time when you felt that God was really showing you what to do? Or perhaps it happened to your dad or mother, or the whole family. Can you think of Bible verses in which God tells you what He wants you to do?

A BIBLE VERSE TO LEARN

Tell me what to do, O Lord. (Psalm 27:11, *TLB*)

LET'S TALK TO GOD

Dear God, thank you for caring about us and what we do. Thank you for the Bible that tells us what you want us to do. Thank you for parents who teach us about you. Help us turn to you when things look too hard or we don't know what to do. We're glad you love us! In Jesus' name, Amen.

NOW FIND THIS STORY IN YOUR BIBLE

It's in Exodus 5:1, 2 and 12:29-42 and 13:21, 22.

STORY 6

THE PEOPLE WHO COULDN'T GO BACKWARDS

Moses and the Hebrew people were free at last. They followed the cloud by day. And they followed the pillar of fire by night. When the cloud stopped—they stopped. And they weren't afraid. They knew that God was with them. They followed that cloud across the desert. They followed it right to the edge of the Red Sea. And then they stopped. In front of them was the Red Sea. On both sides of them were big mountains. There was no place to go but BACKWARDS. But still they weren't afraid. They weren't afraid until—

At first it was just a rumble, like distant thunder. And then it got louder. And then—"It isn't thunder," shouted their guards.

"It's the rumble of chariot wheels!" And the people scrambled out of their tents to listen. The rumble grew louder.

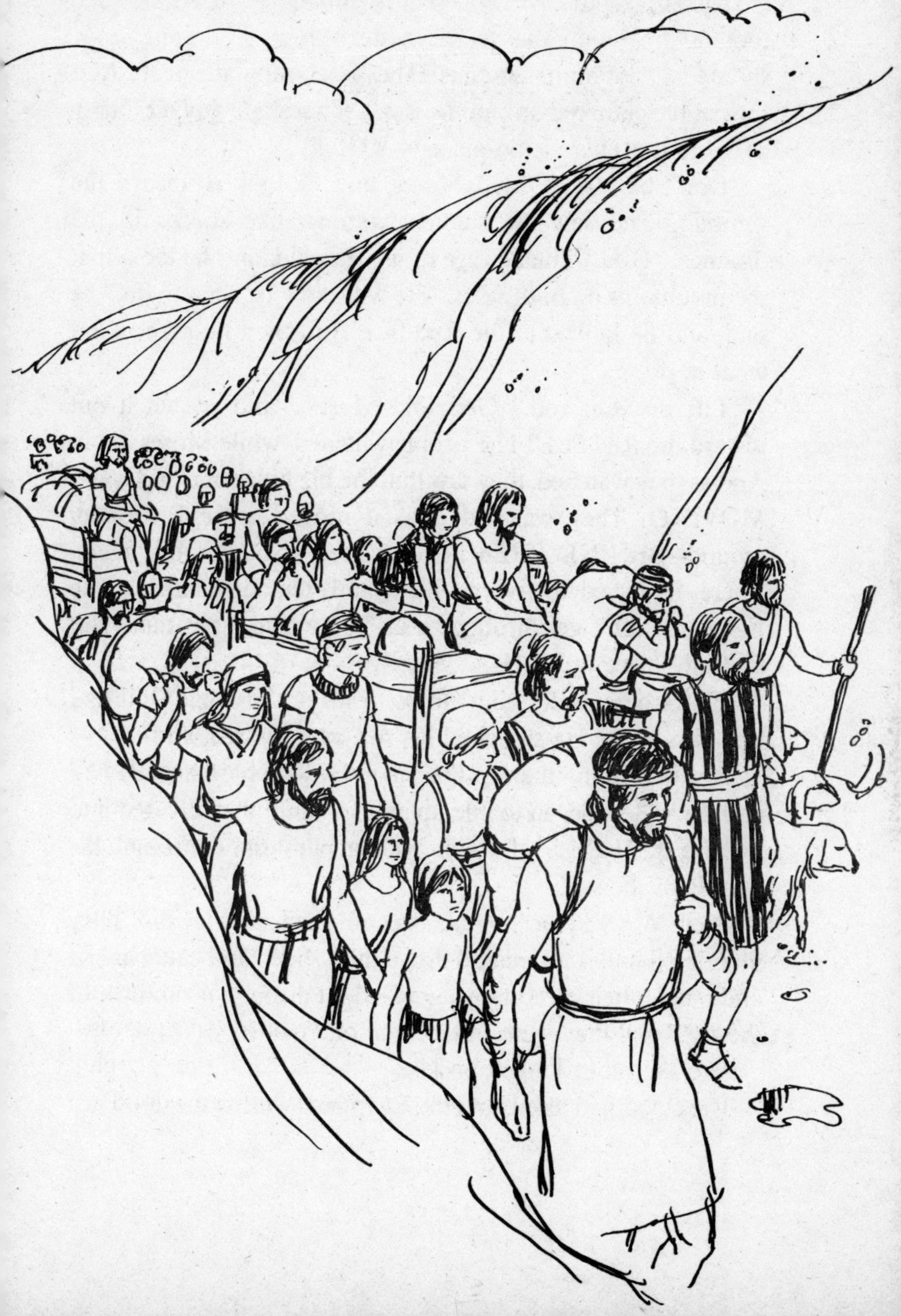

"It's the Egyptians!" they cried. "The wicked Pharaoh has changed his mind again!" And they climbed up on rocks at the foot of the mountains to see better. "It IS Pharaoh!" they shouted. "And all his soldiers! They're coming after us!" And the people gathered around Moses. "What shall we DO?" they asked him. "There is no place to RUN!"

"Don't be afraid," said Moses, and he looked toward the rumbling and saw the soldiers coming, like specks in the distance. "God will take care of us," he said, and he looked at the mountains on both sides. "He will show us what to do," he said, and he looked at the Red Sea. And then he asked God what to do.

"Lift up your rod," God told Moses, "and stretch it out toward the Red Sea." The people watched, while Moses did it. And as they watched, they saw that the big pillar of cloud was—MOVING. They watched it as it moved around, around, around—BEHIND THEM. They waited. It didn't move again. There it stayed—between them and the Egyptians. "The Egyptians can't get through to us," they said, "but there still isn't any place to RUN."

"Don't be afraid," said Moses. And he did what God had told him to do. He stretched his rod over the sea, and—

Wishhhhhhhh—the wind began to blow. It blew and BLEW and the waters began to pile up and UP until they divided into two great WALLS of water with a path right through the middle of the sea!

There WAS a place to run, after all! And run they did. They scrambled and scurried and drove their sheep and cattle ahead and pulled their carts and wagons—right through the middle of the sea, until they were safe on the other side.

And then they looked back.

The cloud had lifted, and the Egyptians were coming—down

to the edge of the water, and through the path, and through the sea—right after them!

Moses acted quickly. As soon as all the Hebrew people were safely across, he stretched out his rod again—And with a mighty ROAR the waters came tumbling, swirling, foaming, back again to cover the path—and the Egyptians disappeared into the sea!

It was all over. The Hebrew people were safe again. Safe from the Egyptians. And the wicked Pharaoh. They gathered there on the shore and thanked God.

Even with the sea in front and the mountains on both sides and the Egyptians in back—God had watched over them every minute.

LET'S TALK ABOUT THE BIBLE STORY

Can you think of any time in your life when things looked absolutely HOPELESS and then, the VERY LAST MINUTE, something happened to make it turn out all right? Do you suppose God had anything to do with it? Did you remember to thank God?

A BIBLE VERSE TO LEARN

With God all things are possible. (Matthew 19:26, *KJV*)

LET'S TALK TO GOD

Dear God, we know that all things are possible with you, that there is nothing you cannot do, and that we should trust you whenever we feel afraid. Thank you for watching over us. In Jesus' name, Amen.

NOW FIND THIS STORY IN YOUR BIBLE

It's in Exodus 14:1-31.

STORY 7

THE GRUMBLE-MUMBLE PEOPLE

Moses and the Hebrew people were safe on the other side of the Red Sea. God had promised to lead them to a wonderful land. But first they had to go through a wilderness. No trees. No gardens. No roads. No houses. No stores. No water. Just wilderness.

They followed the pillar of cloud on—and on—and ON. And after awhile they began to get thirsty. And they began to grumble. "Water!" they cried. Grumble-mumble-grumble. "We should have stayed in Egypt." Grumble-mumble. And then—

"Water!" Someone shouted, up ahead. And they all rushed up ahead, to see. Sure enough, there was water—beautiful, wet water, shining in the sun! They shouted for joy—they ran

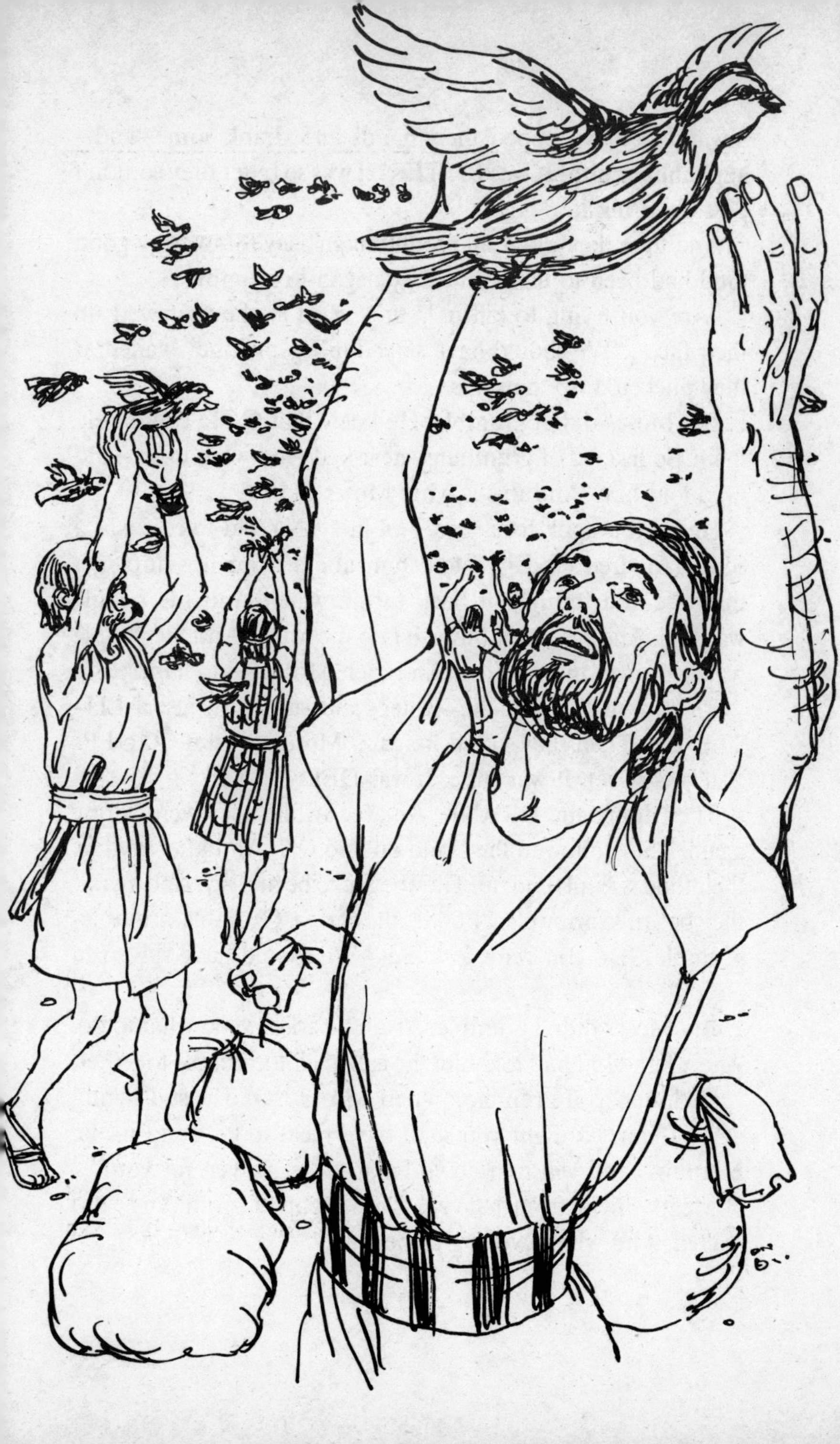

toward it—they cupped their hands and drank some—and—aughhhhhhhhhh! It was BITTER! It was so bitter they couldn't possibly drink it.

And then they did a shameful thing. They forgot how good God had been to them and they began to grumble.

"Are you trying to kill us?" they cried as they screwed up their faces. "We should have stayed in Egypt," they wailed as they puckered up their lips.

But Moses didn't grumble. He knew that GOD could help them. So instead of grumbling, he asked God what to do. And God told him. And this is what Moses did.

He went to look for a tree. Not just ANY old tree. It was a SPECIAL tree God had told him about. And he—hup—got that tree and brought it back to the water. And the people watched. And he—hup! threw it into the water. And the people watched. And they waited. And then Moses said, "Drink!"

They went—up—to—the—water—and—tasted it, just a LITTLE. Slp. Then they tasted it again. More, this time. GULP.

It was sweet. It was pure. It was DELICIOUS!

They drank and DRANK. And for awhile, they were happy again. They followed the cloud on and ON. And after awhile, their food was all used up. They began to be hungry. And again they began to grumble. "Food!" they cried. Grumble-mumble-grumble. "Do you want to kill us? We should have stayed in Egypt!"

But Moses didn't grumble. Again he asked God what to do. And when God had told him, he called all the people together.

"Why do you grumble?" cried Moses. "God is still taking care of you. At night you shall have meat to eat—and in the morning, God will rain down bread from heaven for you!"

Meat! Bread from heaven! They stopped grumbling, and waited. And when evening came—

Suddenly, thousands and thousands of birds, called quail, came flying across the sky. So many of them that they looked like a huge black cloud. And flying so low that the people could reach right up with their hands and catch them! They ate and ATE.

And next morning when they got up—there all over the ground—were little white round things that looked like seeds. "Manna?"* they wanted to know.

"It's the bread from heaven that God promised you," said Moses.

"Manna?" they said, as they tasted it. It was sweet, like little cakes made with honey. "Manna!" they cried, as they gathered it. It was GOOD.

"You must gather only as much as you need each day," said Moses. "And you must gather it early in the morning."

But some of the people disobeyed. "There might not BE any here tomorrow morning," they said. Grumble-mumble. And they gathered a lot extra. But the next day, all that they had left over—was SPOILED.

And some of the people were lazy. "Early in the morning is too EARLY," they said. Mumble-grumble. And they waited till later in the day. But the sun came out and melted the manna—and later in the day—it was GONE.

On the day before the Sabbath, Moses told them they must gather TWICE as much, and God wouldn't let it spoil. For on the Sabbath, God wanted them to rest. Sure enough—it didn't spoil—and sure enough—on the Sabbath, there wasn't any manna on the ground.

And so—even though they were the grumbliest-mumbliest people you could imagine—God took care of them and fed

*Which means "What is it?"

them every day. But they had to follow his instructions and obey him—or they didn't have any food to thank him FOR!

LET'S TALK ABOUT THE BIBLE STORY

Can you think of times when you've grumbled and God has given you something anyhow? Did it make you feel a little sheepish? Can you think of times when there might be a wee little excuse for grumbling? Does the Bible have anything to say about this? (See Philippians 2:14.)

A BIBLE VERSE TO LEARN

In every thing give thanks. (1 Thessalonians 5:18, *KJV*)

LET'S TALK TO GOD

Dear God, we know that everybody grumbles once in awhile, but there's really no excuse for it. Help us to remember that you love us anyhow, whether we grumble or not, but that's STILL no excuse. Help us to be thankful instead. In Jesus' name, Amen.

NOW FIND THIS STORY IN YOUR BIBLE

It's in Exodus 15:22-27 and 16:1-35.

STORY 8

TOO MANY GIFTS

A journey through the wilderness!

And the most wonderful part of that journey was the pillar of cloud. No matter what happened to Moses and the Hebrew people, it was always there. When it moved, they followed it. And when it stopped—they stopped and put up their tents. It was low enough for them to see. But not low enough for them to reach. They couldn't touch it, or get up inside it to see what it was like. It was a great mystery. It looked as if nobody was EVER going to really get close to that cloud. But one day—somebody did! And that somebody was Moses!

It happened this way.

One day, they saw a great mountain in the distance. The pillar of cloud went toward the mountain. Closer, closer. And

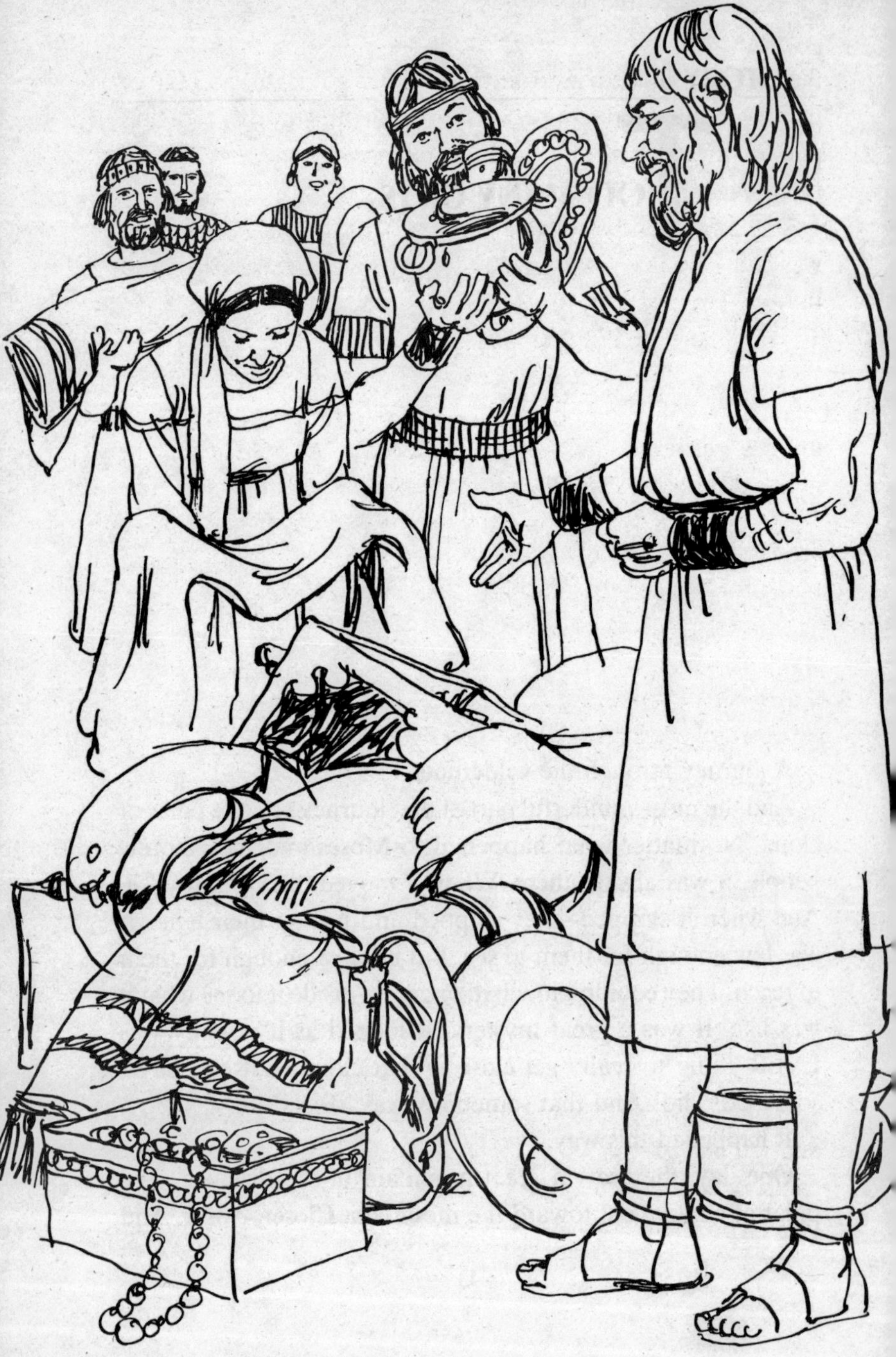

the people followed. And then the cloud got right on TOP of the mountain—and stopped. The people all stopped too, and put up their tents, and camped all around the foot of the mountain. It was Mount Sinai.

One day, after they were all settled, Moses told the people he was going up into the mountain—alone. He said good-by, and they watched him go—

      climbing up, up, UP

          and getting smaller

              and smaller and SMALLER—

until he was just a speck. And then he was gone—swallowed up in the cloud!

Moses was gone for one day—two days—ten days—TWENTY days. What could God be saying to him in all that time? Twenty-five days—thirty days. It must be important. Thirty-five days—FORTY days. And then they saw him coming back.

It WAS important! God wanted them to build a church!

"A tent-church," said Moses. "It's to be called a Tabernacle. And God wants you to bring your gifts to build it. He told me all the things we would need. Are you willing?"

"Yes!" they shouted.

"All right," said Moses. "But God wants gifts only from people who are willing."

"We are willing!" they said, as they remembered the Red Sea and the manna and the cloud and all the things God had done for them. And they hurried to their tents to bring out their gifts.

As the days went by the workmen got to work measuring and cutting boards. And the gifts poured into the center of camp. Gold and silver and rings and bracelets and earrings and pins. And rams' skins and badgers' skins and goats' skins and

goats' hair cloth and red cloth and blue cloth and purple cloth—
"Stop!"

Moses held up his hands to the people. "Stop," he said. "My workmen tell me you are bringing in so many gifts, they cannot use them all! Stop! Don't bring any more!"

And it was true. The gifts were piled so high, there were more than they needed to build their tent-church. And God knew the people loved him. Because every gift was brought by a WILLING giver!

LET'S TALK ABOUT THE BIBLE STORY

What would you do if you'd saved up enough money for a new kite or a new doll and then you found out that your church needed money to build some new rooms? Do you think God would expect you to give all of it? Some of it? How much? What if you gave it all because your mother asked you to, but you weren't really WILLING? What do you really think God expects?

A BIBLE VERSE TO LEARN

God loves a cheerful giver. (2 Corinthians 9:7, *NASB*)

LET'S TALK TO GOD

Dear God, help us to remember that the nicest part about giving is to give CHEERFULLY. And dear God, we thank you for giving US so much! In Jesus' name, Amen.

NOW FIND THIS STORY IN YOUR BIBLE

It's in Exodus 24:15-18 and 25:1-9 and 35:1-35 and 36:1-7.

STORY 9

THE WONDERFUL CHURCH IN THE WILDERNESS

God had done so much for Moses and the Hebrew people. And now at last God had asked them to do something for him. He had asked them to build a church. He had told Moses how he wanted it built—every single detail. And he had asked the people to bring their gifts willingly to build it. And they HAD brought their gifts WILLINGLY, and had piled them up in the center of camp. Now they were ready to get to work.

Of course it had to be a tent-church so the people could pack it up and carry it with them when they moved on. And of course Moses had to tell them just how to build it. "It's going to be a big job," said Moses. "Are you willing?"

"We are willing," they said. And then the excitement began!

The men got busy. They cut boards from acacia trees. They melted the jewelry down to big pots of gold and silver and brass. Some of them covered the boards with gold. Some of them made hooks of silver and bowls of brass. And some of them made a beautiful golden candlestick, and a table and an altar which were covered with gold.

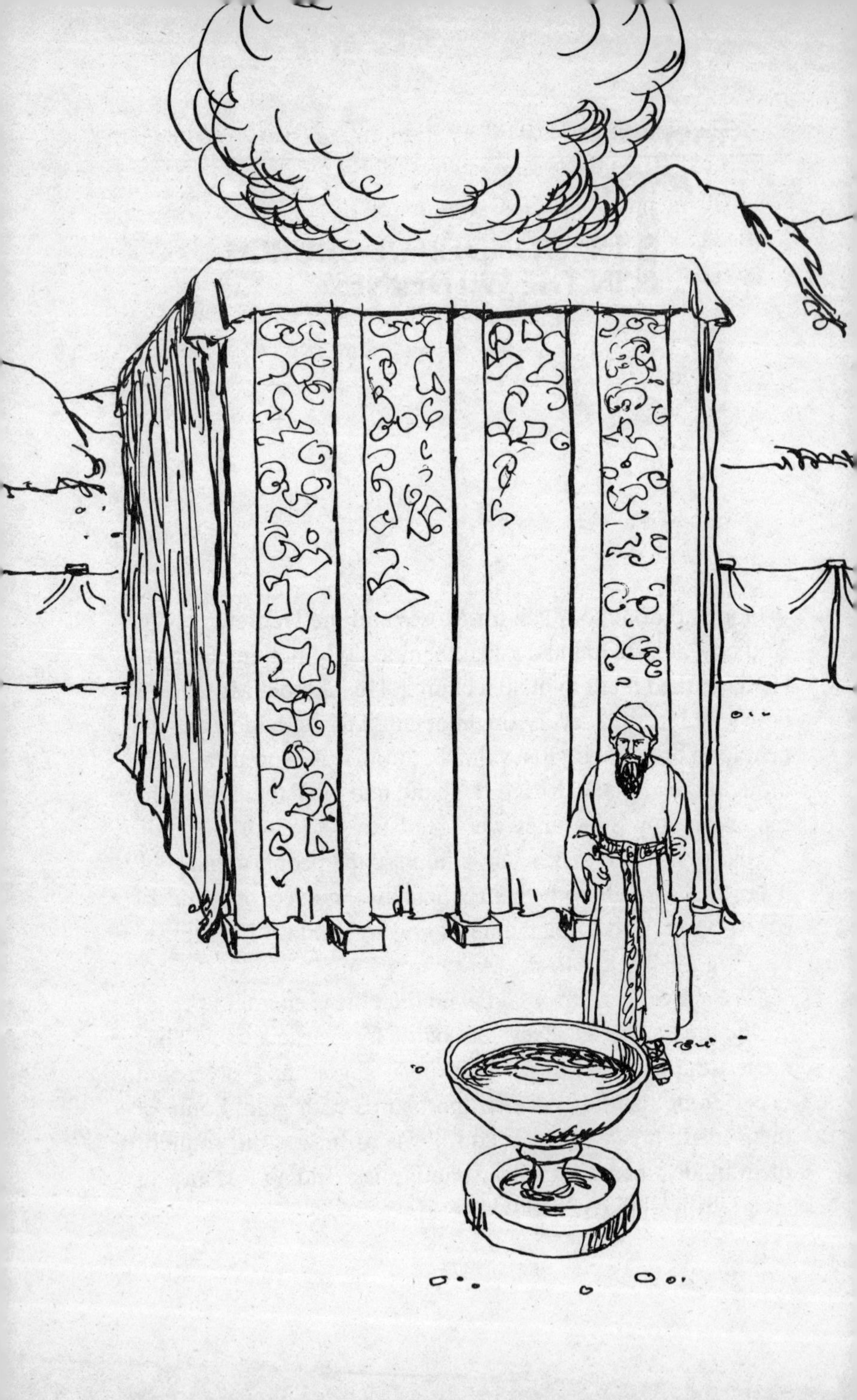

The women got busy. They spun threads of purple and blue and red. They dyed rams' skins red.

The men got busy. They made ENORMOUS curtains—and used the threads of purple and blue and red to make beautiful designs in them.

The children got busy. Some of them carried things to the workmen. Some of them held the cloth for their mothers to sew. And some of them minded their baby brothers and sisters, so they wouldn't get in the way.

EVERYBODY was busy. And everybody was thinking, "Will God be pleased with his new Tabernacle?" They thought about it while they fastened the golden boards together. They thought about it while they hung the beautiful red and purple and blue curtains over the top. And while they put the goats' hair curtains over these to protect them. And the rams' skins over the goats' hair curtains. And the badgers' skins over all, so the rain wouldn't get in.

After the tent-church was all put together, they put the things inside—just the way God told Moses to put them.

First, in went the most special treasure of all. It was a golden box. They called it an Ark. And on the top of the Ark were two golden angels.

Then up went a very special curtain, right in front of the Ark.

And then in went the golden table and the golden altar and the golden candlestick.

And then up went the rest of the curtains. Everything was beautiful!

The whole TABERNACLE was beautiful. They stood back and looked at it. And waited. And wondered. Would God be pleased with it? And then—

The pillar of cloud that was up on top of the mountain began to move. It came down over the camp. Down, down, over the center of the camp, until—

It rested right over the top of the Tabernacle! God was pleased! God was THERE—right in his new tent-church!

And all the people knew that the Tabernacle was the most important part of the camp. It MUST be. GOD was there!

LET'S TALK ABOUT THE BIBLE STORY

What if you had planned to play with your friends all your spare time and then you were asked to do something for your Sunday School class, or your after-school Bible class, or for the closing night of your Vacation Bible School, and it all came crowding in and interfering with your play. Would it be a hard decision for you to make? Do you suppose it might work out if you tried to do a little bit of each? How do you suppose you would figure it out?

A BIBLE VERSE TO LEARN

I was glad when they said to me, "Let us go to the house of the LORD." (Psalm 122:1, *NASB*)

LET'S TALK TO GOD

Dear God, don't ever let us take our church and Sunday School for granted. These people in the wilderness wanted a place to worship so MUCH that they just about wore themselves out building it. And they did it CHEERFULLY. We are glad we have a church where we can meet together to worship you. We want to do all we can to keep it beautiful. In Jesus' name, Amen.

NOW FIND THIS STORY IN YOUR BIBLE

It's in Exodus, chapters 25—27 and chapter 40.

STORY 10

STOP, LOOK AND LISTEN

After the beautiful new tent-church was built, the pillar of cloud came down, down, down, and rested right over the top of it—and STOPPED. And stayed there. And the people knew that meant they were going to stay awhile, too. And they did.

They stayed and stayed and STAYED. Days went by. Weeks went by. MONTHS went by. And if any of the boys or girls said, "When are we going to move on to the land God promised us?" their fathers would say, "Not until the pillar of cloud moves. God says we have to STOP." And so they kept watching the cloud.

It was easy enough to see. Every single person in every part of the camp could see it. And that camp was big. It was bigger than that. It was HUGE. It was as big as a city! But everyone could see the cloud. If the people wanted to obey God, all they had to do was LOOK.

But sometimes Moses wanted to tell them something special.

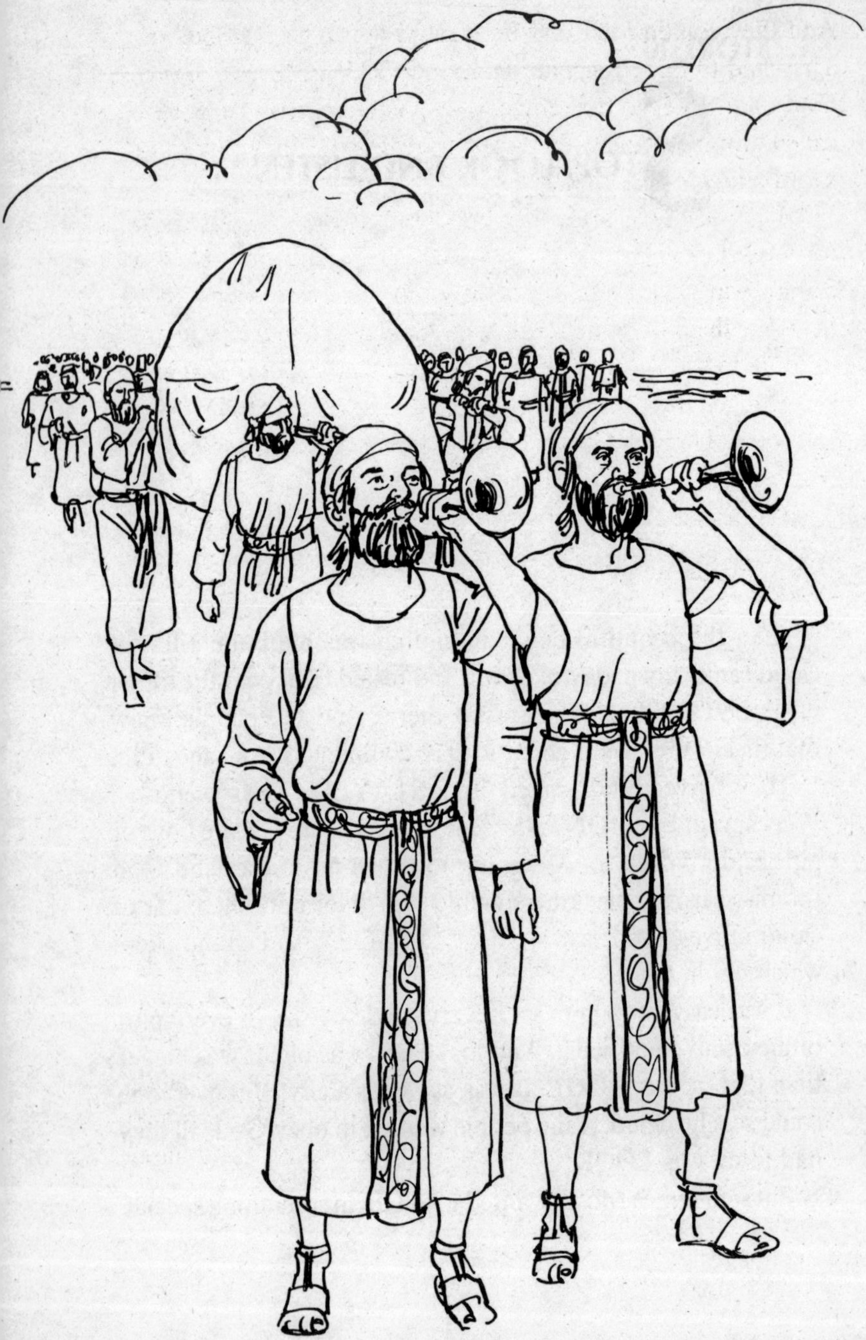

And they couldn't tell that he wanted them, by just looking. They had to have a signal. And God GAVE Moses a signal. God told Moses to make two l-o-n-g silver horns. They were called trumpets and when they were blown, they could be heard all over the camp.

"When you hear these trumpets," said Moses, "you'll know it's important. When they blow like this"—and they blew a certain way—"you'll know there is danger. And when they blow like this"—and they blew another way—"it means you are to come to the Tabernacle. But when the cloud moves again, and you get all packed up to go—and they blow like THIS"—and they blew a very special way—"It means forward—MARCH!"

So even though the camp was HUGE, everybody could hear the trumpets. If the people wanted to obey God, all they had to do was LISTEN. And so the months went by. A whole YEAR went by. And then, one day—

The pillar of cloud began to move! Everybody scurried this way and that. They packed up their tents and all their things. They packed dishes and rugs and clothes and blankets. But the most important thing to pack was the tent-church! They took down the curtains and the animal skins and carefully folded them. They packed the golden candlestick and the brass bowls and the table and the altar—everything! They unfastened the golden boards and put them in carts.

And last of all, they covered up the beautiful golden Ark with the angels on top. They covered it with the very special curtain that had been hanging inside the tent-church. Then they covered over that with badgers' skins. Then they covered over THAT with a blue, blue cloth. Then four men—hup—lifted it up and carried it very carefully on their shoulders. And then they listened.

And then—
The trumpets!
They blew a l-o-n-g "forward—MARCH!"

And everybody knew it was time to go! On they marched, through the wilderness. They knew that God was with them. For the pillar of cloud was there, and the trumpets were there—and all they had to do was STOP—LOOK—AND—LISTEN!

LET'S TALK ABOUT THE BIBLE STORY

Can you think of some of the signals in school that you have to obey in order to get along? How about at home? Which ones are you supposed to listen for? Which ones are you supposed to look for? What are the signals God gives us today, so we can follow him? What Book are these signals in?

A BIBLE VERSE TO LEARN

Follow God's example in everything you do. (Ephesians 5:1, *TLB*)

LET'S TALK TO GOD

Dear God, sometimes signals and bells and things like that are a nuisance because they make us stop and do something when we'd rather be doing something else. Help us to remember that when we're obeying our parents and teachers and other people who are in authority over us,* we're really following GOD. And thank you for the Bible that tells us what you want us to do. In Jesus' name, Amen.

NOW FIND THIS STORY IN YOUR BIBLE

It's in Numbers 9:15-23 and 10:1-13.

---

*People who are bosses over us.

STORY 11
TWO AGAINST TEN

You know how it is, when you're waiting for something wonderful to happen. Like your birthday. You wait and wait and WAIT—and you think it's NEVER going to come—and then, suddenly—there it is!

That's the way it was with the Hebrew people. Moses and the people marched and stopped and marched again and waited and WAITED. And then, suddenly—there it was! The Promised Land. Just a few miles away!

The pillar of cloud stopped. The people stopped. They put up their beautiful Tabernacle, and unpacked their things—and waited for God to tell them what to do. And he did.

"God has told me to send spies into the land," Moses told them.

Spies?

"Yes," said Moses, "I'm going to send twelve spies to look over the land and come back and tell us what they saw."

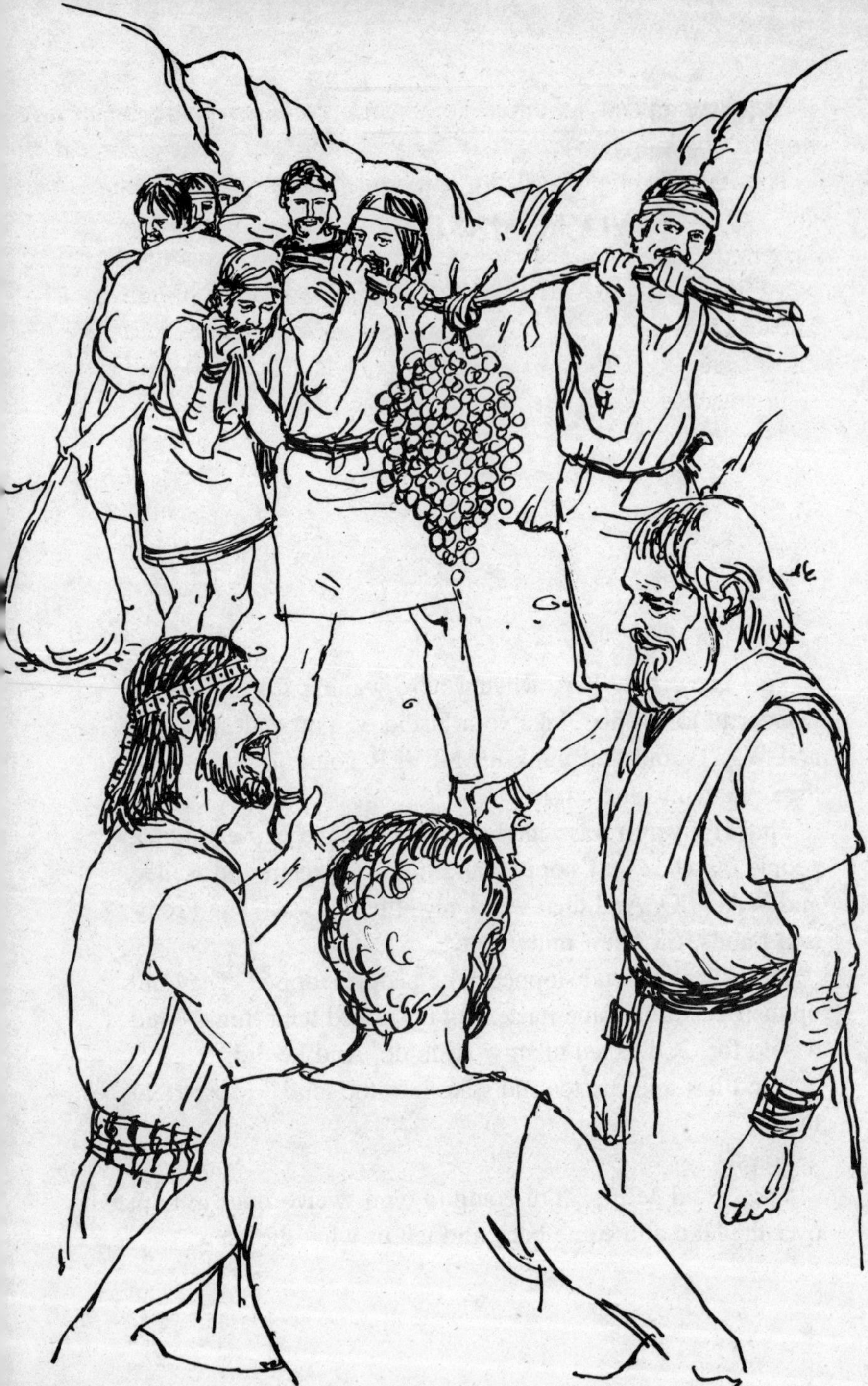

Everyone talked at once. Spies—into the new land! It wouldn't be long now!

They talked about it while Moses chose twelve strong men to go. They talked about it while they gathered around the Tabernacle to ask God to be with them. They talked about it while the twelve men said good-by to their families and started off. And they were still talking about it when the men left, and disappeared—just specks in the distance. The Promised Land!

The people could hardly wait.

They looked and listened and talked about it. Ten days went by. What would the men find? Twenty days went by. How would they be treated? Thirty days went by. What would they have to tell when they got back? Thirty-five days went by. What if they DIDN'T come back? Ohhhhhhhh. Forty days went by. And then—

"They're coming, they're coming!" The shout went up all over the camp. And sure enough—first just specks in the distance—and then—the men—all twelve of them. They were safe! The people gathered around.

"There is fruit in the land," the spies said, and they swung a big pole off their shoulders with a bunch of grapes tied to it—nearly as big as a wheelbarrow! "There are figs and pomegranates too," they said, and they took fruit out of their packs such as the people had never seen before. "And there's grass—and water—and grain—everything!" they said—"BUT—!"

Everybody was quiet. Ten of the spies scowled. "We can't go," they said.

Can't go? The people's hearts almost stopped.

"We can't go over," the men went on. "The people are strong and BIG—almost like GIANTS. And their cities have high walls that nearly reach to the sky. They'll kill us all. We can't go over!"

"Wait!"

It was the two other spies. Their names were Joshua and Caleb. "Wait!" they said, and they held up their hands. The people listened.

"We CAN go!" said Caleb. "God is with us. We needn't be afraid. Let's go!"

"No!" shouted the other spies.

"God will help us!" said Joshua and Caleb.

And the ten spies shouted and the people shouted, until you couldn't hear Joshua or Caleb at all.

"We can't go!" shouted the ten spies. And the people answered, "That's right! We can't go!"

And they didn't.

Those foolish people stayed in the wilderness. They stayed for years and YEARS. There was the Promised Land they'd been waiting for—but they didn't go over because they were afraid. And there was God, waiting to help them—but they didn't let him—because they didn't believe!

LET'S TALK ABOUT THE BIBLE STORY

How do you think YOU would have felt if you heard the spies say there were people like giants in the new land? Have you ever been afraid? When? Did you ask God to help you? How did God answer your prayer?

A BIBLE VERSE TO LEARN

God said, *'Do not fear, for I am with you; . . . I will help you.'* (Isaiah 41:10, *NASB*)

LET'S TALK TO GOD

Dear God, we know it's not a sin to be afraid, but it IS a sin not to believe you will help us when you say you will. The whole idea is to ask you to give us the courage to do what is RIGHT. We thank you for your loving care. In Jesus' name, Amen.

NOW FIND THIS STORY IN YOUR BIBLE
It's in Numbers 13:1-33 and 14:1-38.

STORY 12

More Grumble-Mumbles

No Promised Land! And all because the people didn't believe God could take care of them. The people of Israel turned back to the wilderness. And Moses turned sadly back with them.

God was still with them. The pillar of cloud was still there, and the tent-church was still there, and the manna was still there—but they weren't happy. They wandered from place to place in the wilderness, not getting anywhere, because they hadn't gone to the one place God had wanted them to go. And then—they got the mumble-grumbles again!

It started with LITTLE mumbles. "Nothing but manna, day after day," they mumbled to themselves. And they thought of the figs and other fruit and that big bunch of grapes on the pole.

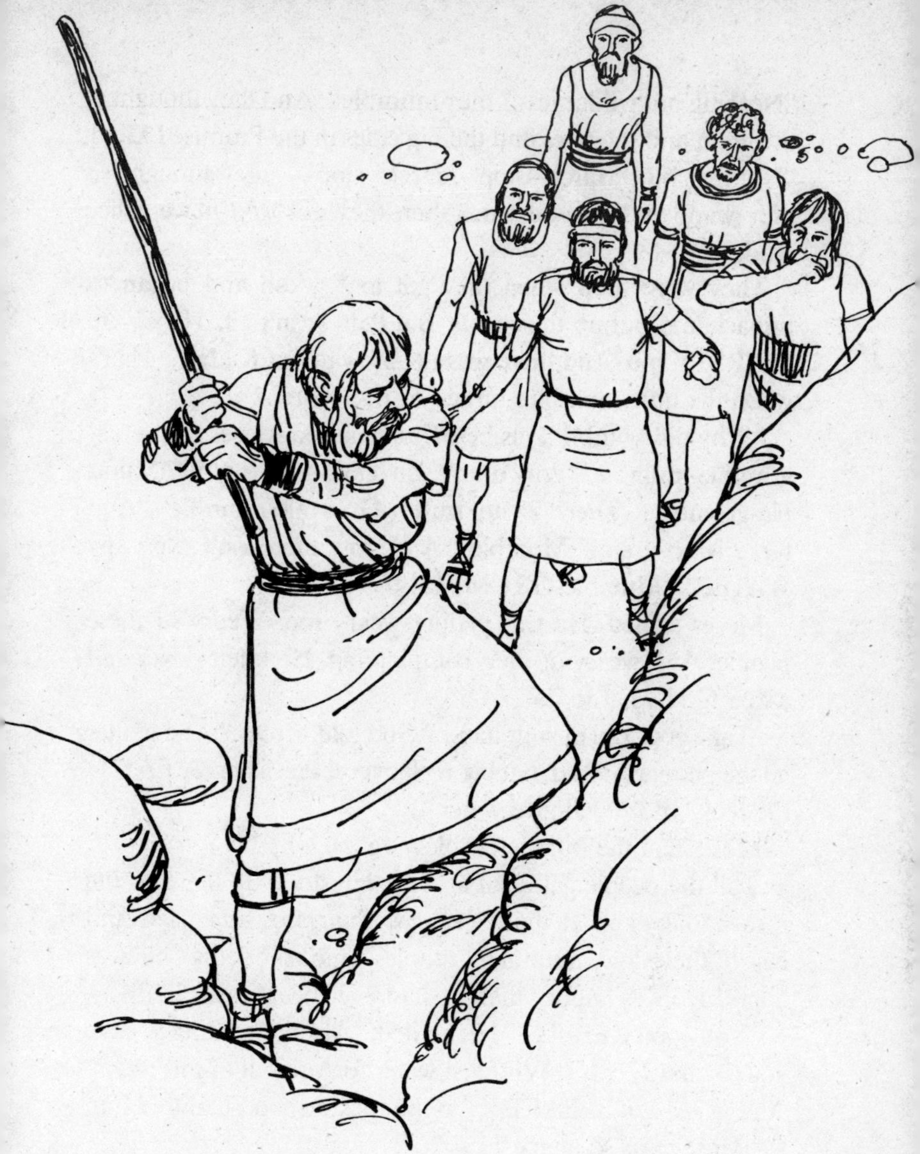

"Nothing but wilderness," they mumbled. And they thought of the grain and the trees and the big cities in the Promised Land. "Nothing but 'March—stop—march—stop!' " they thought, as they wandered around. And then they got to a place called Kadesh.

They were tired when they got to Kadesh and began to unpack and put up their tents. But that wasn't all. They were THIRSTY too. And there wasn't any water at Kadesh. That's when the little mumbles turned to BIG ones.

"Why did you bring us here?" they asked Moses. Mumble-grumble-mumble. "Why didn't you leave us in Egypt?" Mumble-grumble. "There is no fruit." Grumble-mumble. "And there is no grain." Mumble. "And now there isn't even any WATER!" Mumble-GRUMBLE.

Moses sighed. He was getting weary too. Weary of these people. And weary of their complaining. He knelt down and asked God what to do.

"Take your rod in your hand," God told Moses. "And gather all the people around that big rock over there. Then SPEAK to the rock, and it will give water."

Moses had the trumpeters blow on the long silver trumpets, and all the people gathered around. He stood up there by the rock and looked at them. He saw their scowling faces and heard their low mumble-grumbles—and suddenly—he was angry! He was angrier than he had ever been in his life!

"You—you REBELS!" he shouted. "Always wanting to have your own way. Must WE fetch water for you out of this rock?" And instead of SPEAKING to the rock, as God had told him to—Moses was so angry, he—
WHAM!
—took his rod and STRUCK the rock with all his might!

Oh—oh—OH. He'd said, "Must WE fetch water?" when it was GOD who was fetching the water. That was the worst thing he could have said. And he'd STRUCK the rock when God told him to SPEAK to it. That was the worst thing he could have done.

But, in a minute—

—the most wonderful thing happened!

Out of the rock—swirling, bubbling, foaming, tumbling—came—WATER! God had kept his promise!

The people cupped their hands and drank it. They filled their jugs with it. They splashed it over their faces and necks and arms.

WATER! It just kept coming out of that big rock. It kept coming and coming and COMING. Until there was enough for everybody.

But the people weren't very happy. Because they knew they had the grumble-mumbles in their hearts.

And Moses wasn't very happy, either. Because he knew that he had disobeyed God.

LET'S TALK ABOUT THE BIBLE STORY

God told Moses to do one thing and Moses did another. What was it? God sent the water all right, but Moses still wasn't happy. Why? And the people weren't really happy either. Why? Can you think of a time when you were told to do one thing and you did another? How did it turn out? How did it make you feel?

A BIBLE VERSE TO LEARN

Jesus said, *"If you love Me, you will keep My commandments."* (John 14:15, *NASB*)

LET'S TALK TO GOD

Dear God, help us to remember that to obey means to do something EXACTLY as we are told—not just any old wishy-washy way. And keep us from the mumble-grumbles so we won't make everybody miserable. We thank you for loving us. In Jesus' name, Amen.

NOW FIND THIS STORY IN YOUR BIBLE

It's in Numbers 20:1-13.

STORY 13

THE LAWS THAT LASTED FOREVER

Now a lot of important things happened to Moses and his people as they wandered through the wilderness, but one of the most IMPORTANT things, was what happened in this story.

It was BEFORE the spies went into the Promised Land. And before Moses whammed the rock.

Do you remember way back when Moses came down from that huge mountain* and told the people God wanted them to build a tent-church? Well, God wanted them to do something else, too. And this is what it was.

"You know how good God has been to us," said Moses. "He has helped us every time we've been in trouble. NOW—"

"Now—WHAT?" the people wondered.

*Mount Sinai

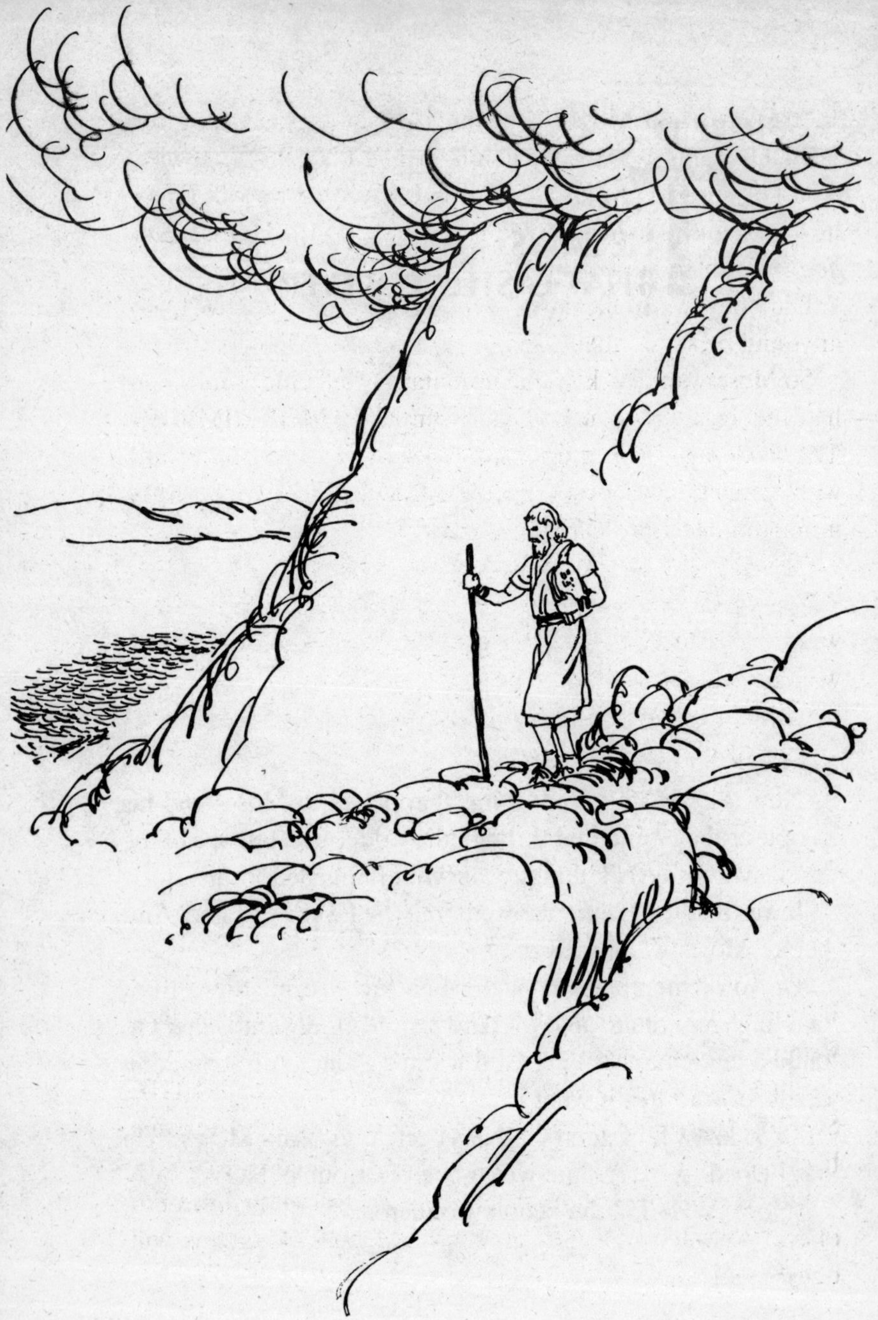

"NOW—" said Moses, "he wants US to do something for HIM. He wants us to belong to him in a VERY SPECIAL way. And he wants to give us a SET OF LAWS—so we will know how he wants us to live. And you may have your CHOICE. Do you want these laws or not?"

Did they want the laws? Oh YES! "Tell God we'll do anything he says!" they cried.

So Moses went back up the mountain to tell God. And when he came back down he had something even MORE IMPORTANT to say. "You must get all cleaned up," he said, "and wash your clothes. For in three days God is coming right to the mountain. He'll be RIGHT HERE."

Oh MY!

Everybody got busy at once. They cleaned the camp. They washed their clothes. They washed themselves. And then they waited. And sure enough—

On the morning of the third day, suddenly—

> The lightning FLASHED!
> The thunder CRASHED!
> A mysterious trumpet BLEW!
> And the mountain SHOOK!
> And SMOKED!
> And TREMBLED!

The people trembled too. They backed up and BACKED UP—until they were a safe distance away. And there they waited—frightened.

But Moses went right up into the mountain and INTO THE SMOKE, to get the set of laws from God. And when he came back—

Sure enough, he told them all the laws God wanted them to obey. "We will obey!" they shouted. "All that God says we will obey!"

And do you know, those laws have lasted right up until today—for they are the TEN COMMANDMENTS we have in the Bible! They are lasting forever—or at least until Jesus comes back again!

LET'S TALK ABOUT THE BIBLE STORY

Does God give us rules and laws to make us miserable? Think of some commands God has given us in the Bible. Then think about why he gave them. What are some rules you have at home? At school? At church? If you love God, what will you do about rules and laws and commandments?

A BIBLE VERSE TO LEARN

The law of the LORD is perfect. (Psalm 19:7, *KJV*)

LET'S TALK TO GOD

Dear God, you are so good to us! One of the most wonderful things you do for us is to give us rules and laws to obey for our own good. Help us to obey cheerfully. In Jesus' name, Amen.

NOW FIND THIS STORY IN YOUR BIBLE

It's in Exodus, chapter 19:1-20.

NOW FIND THE TEN COMMANDMENTS IN YOUR BIBLE

They are in Exodus 20:1-17.

Psalm 86:5

O Lord, You are so great, You are so good and kind.
O Lord, You are so great, You are so good and kind.
O Lord, You are so great, You are so good and kind.
Lord, You are al-ways read-y to for-give.

Words: Based on Psalm 86:5. Music: Traditional.

PART TWO
STORIES OF JESUS

STORY 14

THE GREATEST PROMISE IN THE WORLD

Once a long, long time ago, the greatest gift in the WORLD was promised. Can you imagine a gift so great and so important that it changed the whole world?

Well, there was a gift just that important. It was a gift God had promised to send to the world.

It wasn't a palace.
It wasn't gold.
It was—A BABY!
A very special baby—God's own son, the baby Jesus.

It was promised to a young woman named Mary. And to a kind man named Joseph. And this is how it all happened.

Mary and Joseph lived in Bible times when angels some-

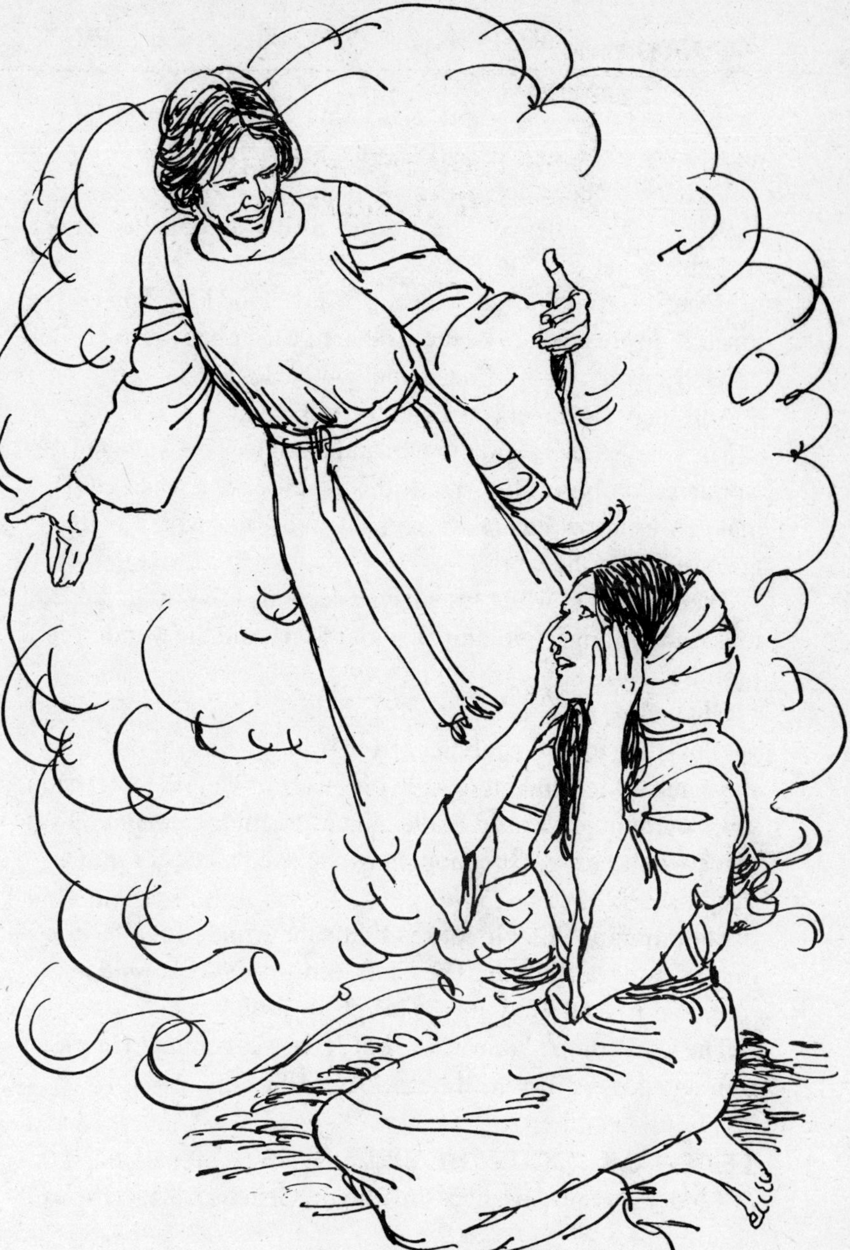

times spoke to people. They don't NOW. But they did THEN.

And one day Mary was praying to God. She didn't know there was going to be a gift. She didn't expect an angel. She didn't even expect a PROMISE. But SUDDENLY—

An angel! Right there before her eyes!

Mary was frightened. She'd never SEEN an angel before. And this angel was SPEAKING to her!

"Don't be afraid, Mary," the angel said. "God loves you very much. You are going to be the mother of a dear baby boy. He'll be God's own son. And his name will be Jesus."

And then the angel was gone. Just like that!

Mary stayed there and thought and thought. This was a most wonderful promise. GOD made this promise. And when GOD makes a promise, he always keeps it. Why, this would be the greatest gift in the world!

Then one night while Joseph was sleeping. HE saw an angel too! And the angel told him all about Mary and the wonderful promise.

Oh, joy!

"I'm going to be the mother of a baby boy," Mary thought as she made some blankets to keep him warm. "He will be God's son," she thought as she made clothes for him to wear. "His name will be Jesus," she thought as she fixed a bed for him to sleep in.

So Mary and Joseph got ready for the wonderful gift. For they knew it was coming. They had seen an ANGEL. God had promised it. And God always keeps his promises.

The world didn't know it yet, but Jesus was coming! He was coming all right! For he'd been PROMISED!

LET'S TALK ABOUT THE BIBLE STORY

Find these promises in the Bible: Genesis 28:15; Psalm

121:3; Isaiah 41:10; Jeremiah 33:3; Romans 8:28; Philippians 4:19.

God's promise to send his son was the most wonderful promise of all. Do you know why? (See John 3:16.)

Aren't you glad God always keeps his promises? How can you thank him for this?

A BIBLE VERSE TO LEARN

Not one word has failed of all (God's) wonderful promises. (1 Kings 8:56, *TLB*)

LET'S TALK TO GOD

Dear God, we're certainly glad to know that when you make a promise you always keep it. Help us to remember this and to believe you. And help us to keep OUR promises too! In Jesus' name, Amen.

NOW FIND THIS STORY IN YOUR BIBLE

It's in Luke 1:26-38 and Matthew 1:18-25.

STORY 15

THE PROMISE COMES TRUE

God had made Mary and Joseph a promise. Not an ordinary promise. It was an EARTH-SHAKING promise. He promised them a very special baby—God's own son, the baby Jesus.

Imagine!

Of course, Mary should go to the very best hospital or maybe even a king's palace for this very special baby to be born. Or stay home and have servants and nurses hurrying and scurrying about, carrying trays and orange juice and sheets and medicine and bumping into each other. And with maids to comb her hair and bathe the new baby and dress him in the finest clothing and brush what little hair he had up to a curl on top and carry him to her bedside and put him gently alongside her, with his tiny head snuggled in the pillow—

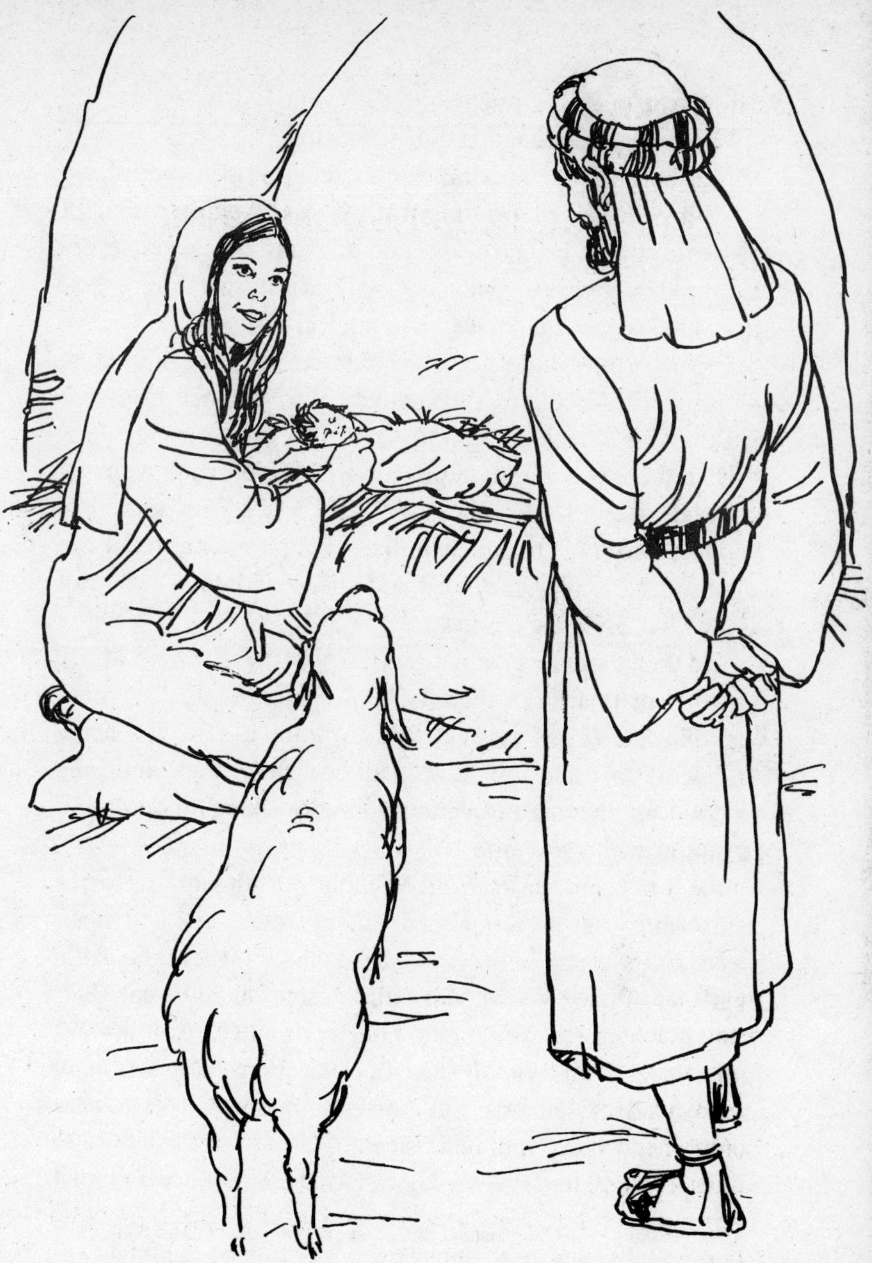

But none of this happened at all.

What really happened is quite amazing.

It all began with the king's order. It tells us in the Bible—". . . there went out a decree from Caesar Augustus, that all the world should be taxed . . . and all went to be taxed, every one into his own city." Which simply meant that Joseph and Mary had to pack up a few belongings on a little donkey, leave their comfortable little house in Nazareth, and clump along bumpy roads—all the way to Bethlehem to pay their taxes and sign the king's book!

Then there was the matter of the crowds. When they finally got to Bethlehem it was just SPILLING OVER with people who had also come to pay their taxes. People and donkeys and camels and bundles and food and sheep and goats—you just can't IMAGINE the confusion!

And then there was the matter of a place to stay. And THAT was the worst part. For there WAS no place to stay. The inns* were filled. EVERY place that had rooms to rent was filled. And poor Mary and Joseph went all over Bethlehem, knocking on doors and getting turned away and knocking on doors and getting turned away until—

One innkeeper said, "Wait!" He had just thought of something. And what he thought of was not nice beds and clean sheets and a warm bath. It was a STABLE—where the cattle slept! And that is where Mary and Joseph finally went. And that was where, that very night, God's promise came true—and the baby Jesus was born. Instead of clean sheets there was straw and instead of servants and nurses and doctors there were donkeys and sheep and cows sleeping.

Yes, there baby Jesus was born. And there, Mary wrapped

---

* An inn is like a motel only instead of having cars, the people had donkeys or camels to park out in a stable.

him in soft clean cloth and laid him—oh so carefully—on some clean straw, in a manger.*

It might SEEM that everything had gone wrong. But actually everything had gone exactly as God wanted it to go.

Jesus had been promised. And now he was HERE!

LET'S TALK ABOUT THE BIBLE STORY

Just imagine how different the world would be if God hadn't kept his promise. Can you think of some ways in which it would be different? Can you think of some ways you can thank God for keeping this great promise?

A BIBLE VERSE TO LEARN

He (God) *loved us, and sent his son.* (1 John 4:10, *KJV*)

LET'S TALK TO GOD

Dear God, we thank you that you loved us so much that you sent us the Lord Jesus to be our Saviour. It sure was a great promise and we're glad you kept it. In Jesus' name, Amen.

NOW FIND THIS STORY IN YOUR BIBLE

It's in Luke 2:1-7.

---

* A manger is a long box to hold the animals' food.

STORY 16

THE STRANGEST ANNOUNCEMENT IN THE WORLD

When new babies are born—how do people find out about it? On the phone? In an announcement card? Or a letter? Do people call it out from their front porch? Clearly, the very FIRST thing to do is to let everybody know, one way or the other—and as soon as possible!

"A baby!"
"Really?"
"Yes—a boy!"
"How big?"
"Eight and a half pounds!"
"My, a BIG fellow!
How wonderful!"

It's just too important to keep secret!

When Jesus was born, there were no announcement cards sent out. But people found out about it in the strangest ways!

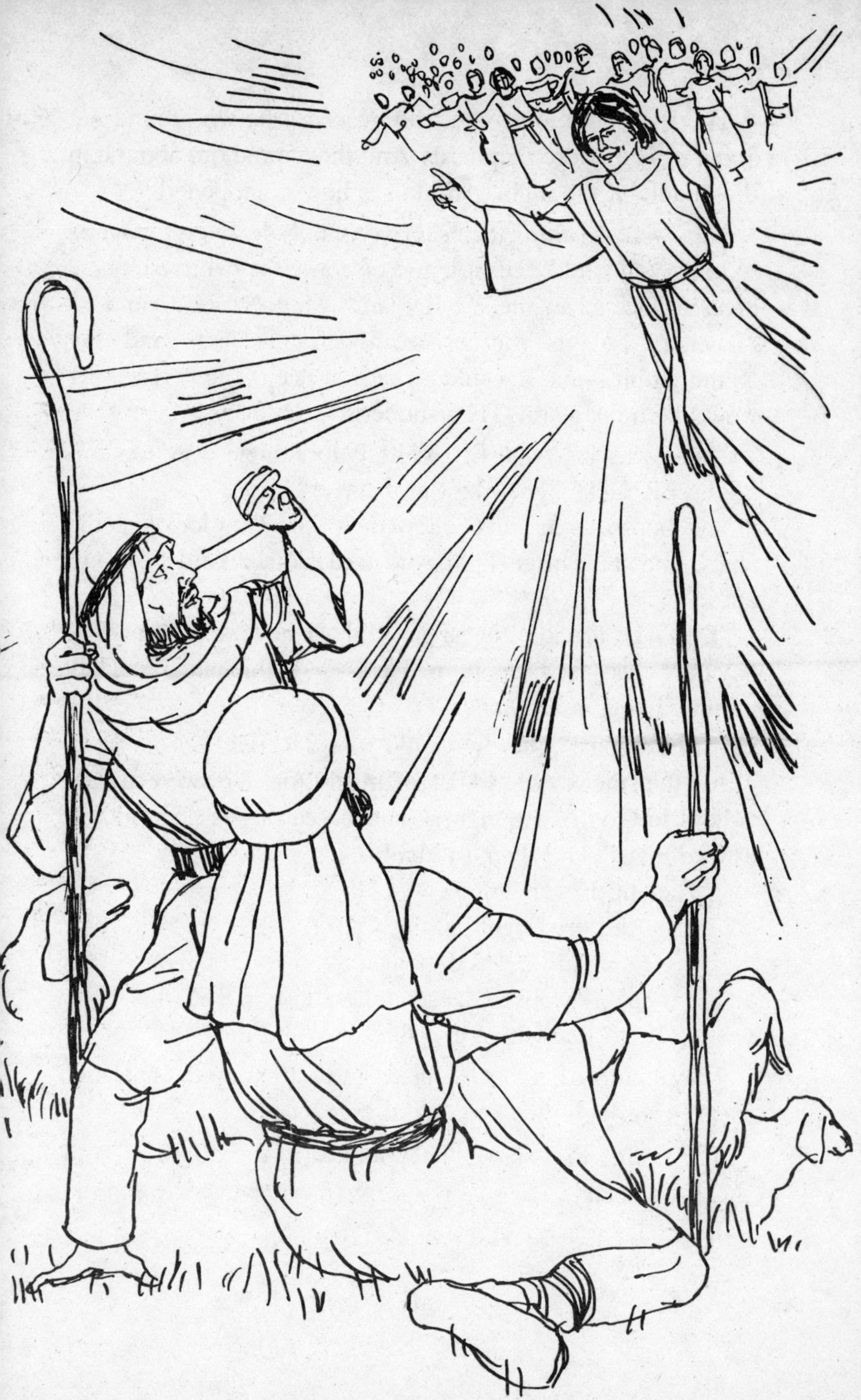

There were some people who lived nearby who found out about it. They were shepherds. And they found out about it in the middle of the night. And this is how it happened.

They were watching their sheep on a hillside. Everything was so quiet you could hear a blade of grass if it twittered in the breeze. Once in awhile, a baby lamb would wake up and go "Baaaaa"—but its mother would lick its ears and say "Shhhhhhhh"—and it would go back to sleep. Then everything would be quiet again. Then suddenly—

There was an ANGEL—right before their eyes! And a bright, BRIGHT light—right in the sky!

The shepherds couldn't believe their eyes. They looked at the angel. And at the bright light. And at each other. And they were afraid.

"Don't be afraid," the angel said. "I have good news! A Saviour* has just been born. He is in Bethlehem right this minute. Lying in a manger."

"The Saviour!" Oh joy! Could it be TRUE?

Just then the sky was FULL of angels. And they were saying, "Glory to God in the highest, and on earth peace, good will toward men." And then, suddenly—

The angels were gone.

And the bright light was gone.

And it was dark again.

The shepherds looked at each other. It MUST be true! They would GO to Bethlehem and find out. And they DID.

They stumbled across the fields and puffed up the hills and sneaked through the streets. And then—

They came to a stable. They looked in the doorway. And there was Mary. There was Joseph. There were sheep. And

---

* The Saviour is the Lord Jesus.

goats. And cows. There was a manger with hay in it. And there—all snuggled in the straw—was baby Jesus!

It was true!

Shhhh. They went in quietly. And shhh. They knelt down. And shhh. They thanked God for baby Jesus.

And then they went back to their sheep.

Oh, they were happy! For they had found out about the most important baby that had ever been born. Not by telephone. Not by an announcement card. Not by a letter. But by ANGELS—and a light in the sky!

For this was not just ANY baby. This was God's son.

LET'S TALK ABOUT THE BIBLE STORY

Can you think of other ways God might have announced that Jesus was born? Why do you suppose he chose this way? How can you help other people know the good news that God sent his Son to be our Saviour?

A BIBLE VERSE TO LEARN

Today in the city of David* there has been born for you a Savior, who is Christ the Lord. (Luke 2:11, *NASB*)

LET'S TALK TO GOD

Dear God, first you made a promise and then you kept it and then you TOLD people about it. We certainly thank you for all this. Help us to remember that it's important to tell people about that promise and all about how you kept it and everything. In Jesus' name, Amen.

NOW FIND THIS STORY IN YOUR BIBLE

It's in Luke 2:8-20.

* Bethlehem.

STORY 17

TWO DREAMS THAT SAVED A LITTLE CHILD

When new babies are born, how do people find out about it when they live far away? Laurie and Jeff have a brand new baby brother. And they've let everybody know by announcements and cards and phone calls. But grandma and grandpa live way across the ocean in another country and there is only one way to let them know. By a CABLEGRAM! First dad has to write the message on a special paper, then the telegraph company has to phone the message way across the ocean, then it has to be written down again on ANOTHER special paper, then at LAST grandpa and grandma read it. Such a business!

People found out about the birth of Jesus in strange ways, too. There were people who lived nearby who found out about it. They were shepherds. And there were people who lived far

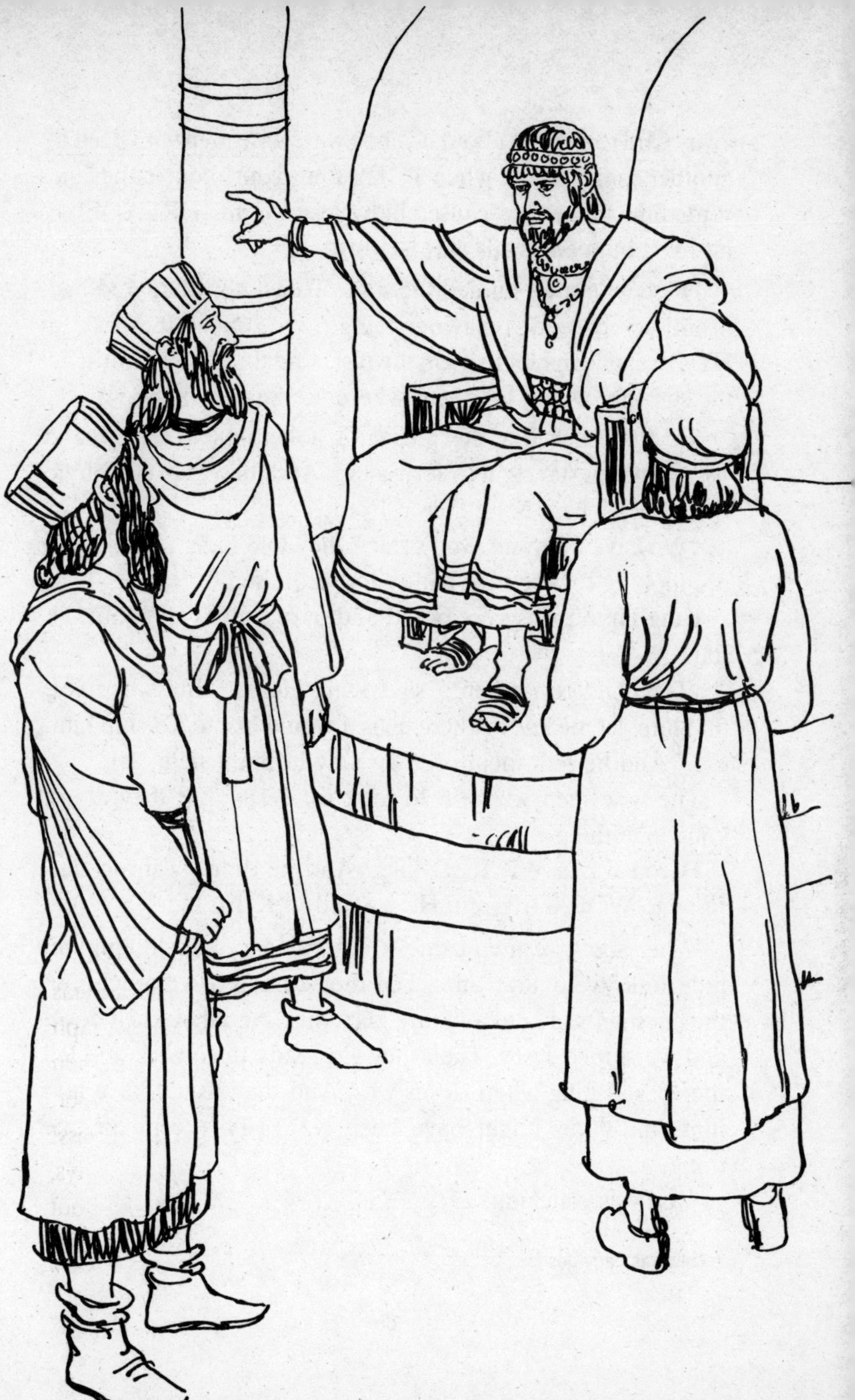

away who found out about it. They were wise men who lived in another country. And when THEY found out about it, they did something that nearly caused baby Jesus harm—DREADFUL harm. It happened this way.

These wise men studied the stars. They knew that God had promised to send a Saviour-King.* One night they saw a HUGE star, brighter than all the rest. And they knew it must be the star that would tell them where the Saviour-King was.

So they packed some gifts and got on their camels and followed that star right to Jerusalem. And they went straight to the palace where King Herod lived.

"We have followed God's star," they told King Herod. "We are looking for the new King God promised."

King Herod was very polite and asked them all about the star.

"The child is not here," said King Herod. "But when you find him, let me know where he is. I would like to worship him, too." And he sent them on their way to Bethlehem.

The wise men went on to look for Jesus. But they didn't know one thing—

Herod was a WICKED king. And he didn't want to find Jesus to WORSHIP him. He wanted to KILL him!

When the wise men came to where Mary and Joseph and little Jesus were, they unpacked their camels and brought out the finest gifts of gold and rare perfumes. And they knelt down and worshiped Jesus. Then they got ready to go back and tell the wicked king where Jesus was. And they would have told him, and Jesus might have been KILLED—except for one thing.

God was watching!

---

* This was baby Jesus.

That night in a dream, God told the wise men, "Do not go back to wicked King Herod. He doesn't want to worship Jesus. He wants to have him KILLED. Go back to your own country."

And the wise men did!

But King Herod was angry. He called his soldiers. "Go to Bethlehem," he told them, "and find this child—I want to have him killed!"

But God was still watching!

At night, in a dream, God told Joseph to take Mary and Jesus and run away. Mary and Joseph packed up their things and wrapped up little Jesus, and stole out of the city and across the desert until they got to Egypt, a country faraway.

And when the soldiers got to Bethlehem and looked in all the places where there were little children so they could kill baby Jesus—he was gone!

King Herod never found Jesus. And Mary and Joseph didn't bring him back until the wicked king was dead. No harm could come to God's son. Because God was watching!

LET'S TALK ABOUT THE BIBLE STORY

Phew! That was close, wasn't it? They didn't have cablegrams and telegrams and phones back in those days, but God used other ways to announce Jesus' birth, and other ways to SAVE Jesus when his life was in danger. What were they? What are some ways God protects YOU from danger?

A BIBLE VERSE TO LEARN

The LORD is your keeper. (Psalm 121:5, *NASB*)

LET'S TALK TO GOD

Dear God, we thank you for taking such good care of Jesus

and for letting the wise men know about him and then we thank you ESPECIALLY for not letting that wicked King Herod go and spoil it all. We thank you for giving us parents and teachers and policemen and all sorts of people to keep us safe. In Jesus' name, Amen.

NOW FIND THIS STORY IN YOUR BIBLE
It's in Matthew 2:1-15.

STORY 18

WHEN JESUS WAS A LITTLE BOY

Even though Jesus was God's own son, he had to grow up just like any other little boy. And God was watching over him every minute.

After the wicked King Herod was dead, and Mary and Joseph and Jesus came back from Egypt—they went to Nazareth to live. Nazareth wasn't a great big city with tall buildings and temples and lots of traffic. It was a little country town, tucked away in the hills.

By this time Jesus wasn't a baby any longer—he was a little boy!

The Bible tells us that he had to learn things. And that he obeyed his mother and Joseph. And that Joseph was a carpenter. So we have a pretty good idea of what Jesus' life was like.

In the morning, the sunshine would sneak in Jesus' window

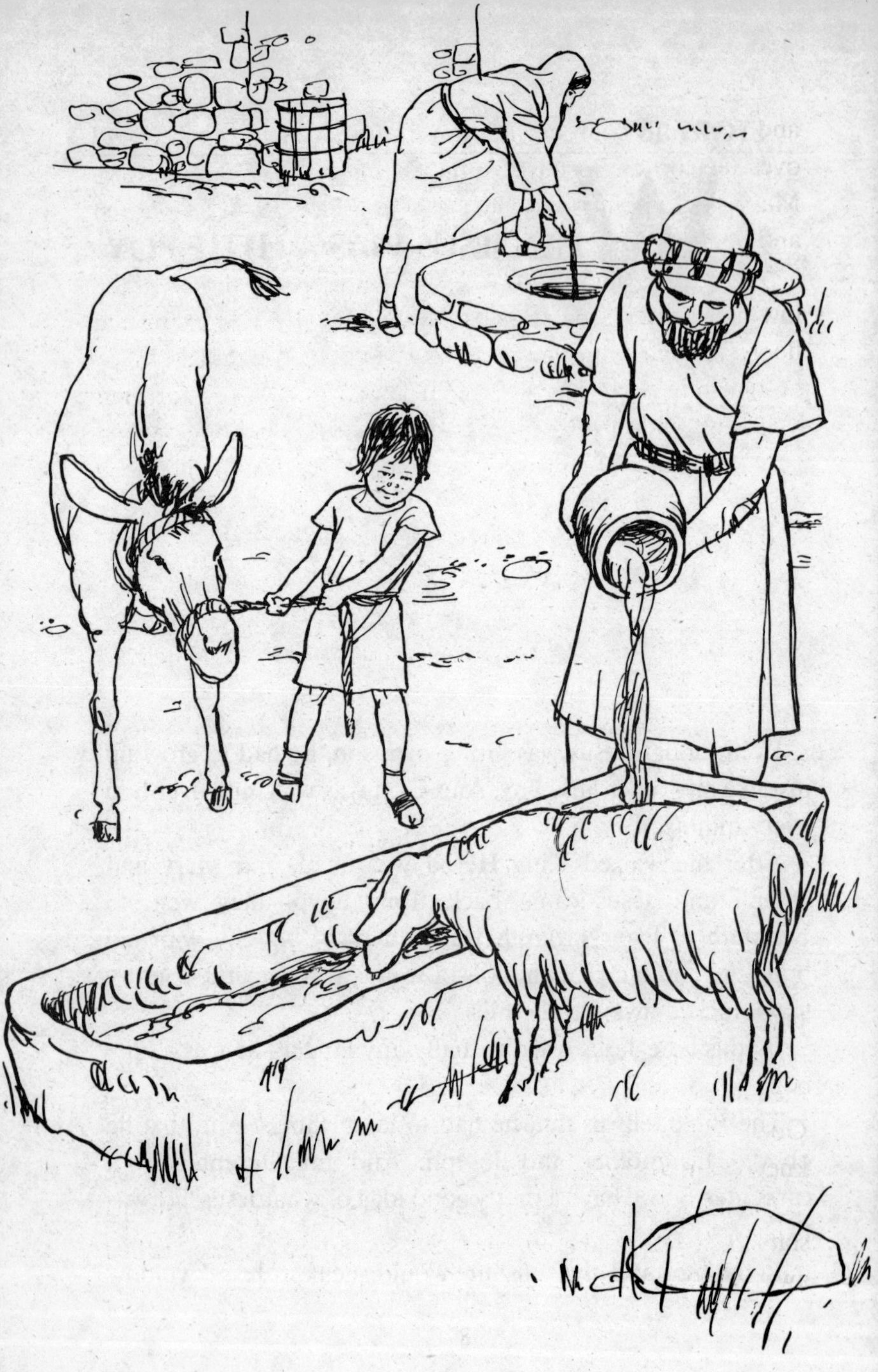

and across his bedroom floor and up the side of his bed and over the top of his covers—and in his eyes—and wake him. Mary would pour water in a basin and help Jesus get washed and dressed. And then it was time for breakfast.

While Mary got breakfast, Jesus would put the dishes on the low bench they used for a table and spread the mats on the floor for them to sit on. Then Mary and Joseph and Jesus sat around on the mats, and Joseph would thank God for their breakfast while they all bowed their heads. Then they would eat barley cakes with fresh butter and honey. And while they ate, they would talk about what they were going to do that day and ask God to help them do everything just right.

There were so many things to do INSIDE their house.

And Jesus helped with everything. He helped feed the animals. He helped Mary get water at the well. And he helped Joseph, too.

He helped Joseph in his carpenter shop. He handed Joseph nails and pieces of wood. He caught the curly shavings as they fell to the floor. And he watched the sawdust sprinkle the floor, like snow, when Joseph went szhhh-szhhh with the saw. And Jesus obeyed Mary and Joseph in everything they asked him to do.

There were so many things to do OUTSIDE their house.

There were walks in the hills and rides on the donkey, and picnics, and friends to play with.

And in the evening Mary and Joseph and Jesus would sit on their doorstep and watch the sun go down—and talk about God. They would tell God's stories over and over, until Jesus knew them all by heart.

And then Jesus would say his prayers and go to bed. And the stars came out—and all of Nazareth would go to sleep, tucked away there in the hills.

That's the way the other people in Nazareth lived. And that's the way Jesus lived, too.

Even though he was God's son, he had to grow up just like any other little boy.

And God was watching over him every minute.

LET'S TALK ABOUT THE BIBLE STORY

What were some of the things Jesus found to do inside his house? Outside? What do you suppose he learned when he helped Joseph and Mary? When he played with his friends? When he went on hikes? When he rode a donkey? When he took care of animals? Do you learn just about the same things today?

A BIBLE VERSE TO LEARN

Children, obey your parents; this is the right thing to do. (Ephesians 6:1, *TLB*)

LET'S TALK TO GOD

Dear God, help us to remember that in everything we do, we are learning something. We learn to be good sports and to be helpful and to obey and to use our muscles when we hike and play outside. Thank you that learning is FUN most of the time, and help us to be good sports when it ISN'T fun. In Jesus' name, Amen.

NOW FIND THIS STORY IN YOUR BIBLE

It's in Luke 2:40 and 52.

STORY 19

WHEN JESUS WAS A BIG BOY

Remember the very first day Mother took you to school? She marched you into the building and up the hall, right into Miss Chalk-dust's room. She introduced you to your teacher and whispered something in your ear about using your handkerchief instead of your sleeve—and then she went HOME—and you were on your own! Oh, joy! Oh, HORRORS! You were half-glad and half-scared. It was all so new! And then, after a while, you got used to it. Remember?

Well, Jesus had to go to school, too. While he was busy helping Mary and Joseph, and learning to obey—he was GROWING. And before he knew it, it was time for him to start going to school.

NOW, things were different. In the morning, when the first rays of the sun s-t-r-e-t-c-h-e-d across his bedcovers and got to his face to wake him, it was more important to get up than ever before.

School!

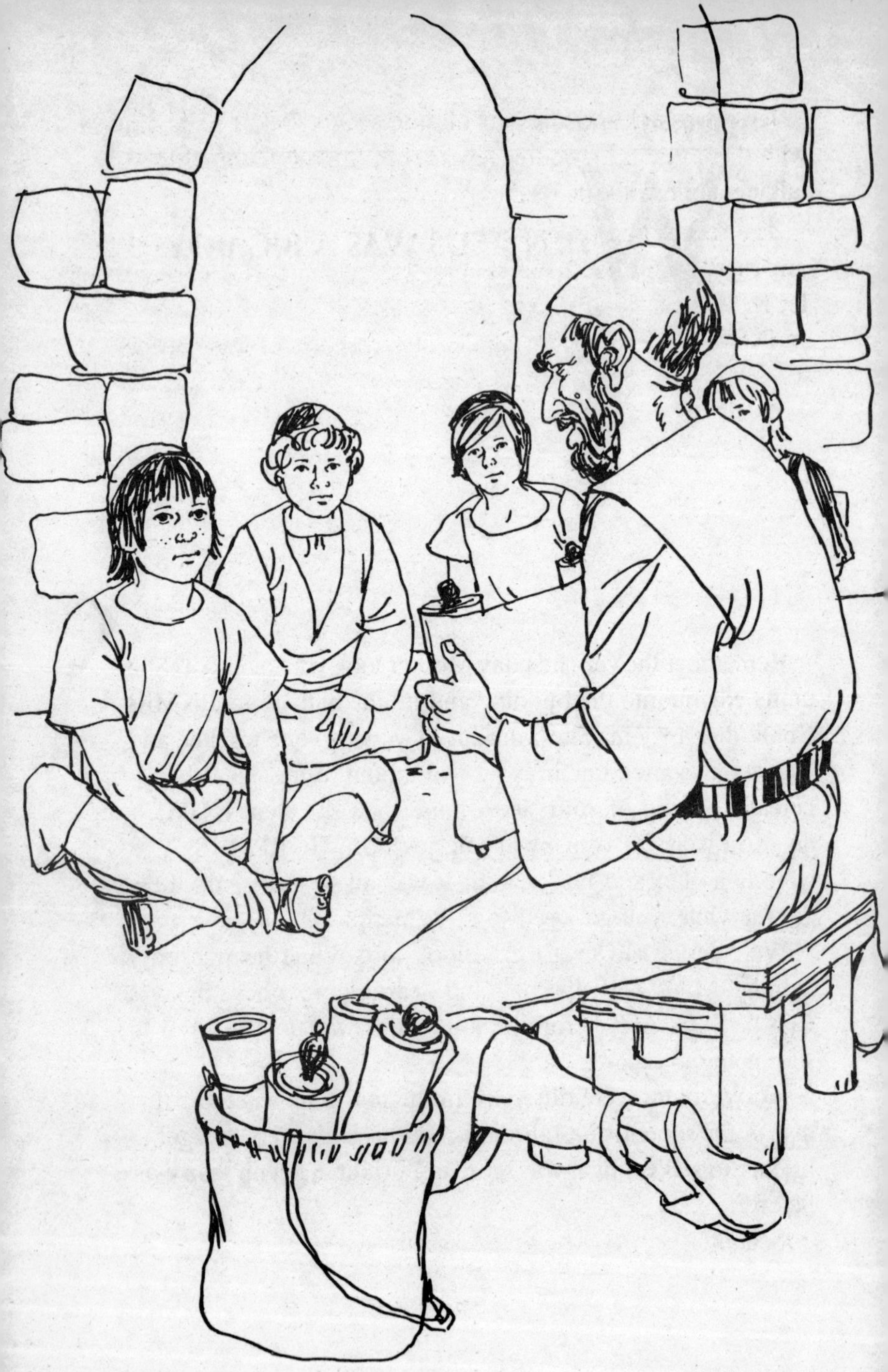

Jesus washed and dressed himself. Mary didn't help him with these things anymore. Jesus spent some time by himself, talking alone with his heavenly Father.

The chores had to be done quickly now. Jesus fed his pets and set the table—and now that he was bigger, perhaps Joseph let HIM thank God for their breakfast!

There wasn't any Miss Chalk-dust, and school wasn't a big building with lots of rooms and desks. The teacher was the MINISTER, and school was in the SYNAGOGUE.* And everything was different. Jesus had to get used to it, the same as you had to get used to your school. He sat on the floor, cross-legged, along with the other boys, and learned.

Jesus learned God's Word. He learned to read from a long strip of paper with a stick at each end. He u-n-r-o-l-l-e-d it and read it, and r-o-l-l-e-d it up again on the other stick. It was called a scroll.

Jesus listened to everything the teacher said, and then said it over and OVER until he knew it by heart. There was so much to learn.

Some things were easy. Some things were hard, and Jesus bowed his head and asked God to help him.

And when he got home, he told Mary all the new things he had learned.

And when Mary and Joseph and Jesus sat on their doorstep in the evening, to watch the sun go down, sometimes Joseph let HIM tell the Bible story.

Oh, yes, things were different now.

Everything was more exciting. Everything was more important. Even though Jesus was God's own son, he went to school and LEARNED things. Just like any other boy!

---

* A synagogue is a place of worship just as your church is.

LET'S TALK ABOUT THE BIBLE STORY
What are some of the things Jesus could do for himself now, that Mary used to help him with? What was the most important thing he learned at school? What are some of the things YOU do for yourself now that you used to have help with? Think about some of the NEW things you've learned in just the past year. Doesn't it make you feel OLD?

A BIBLE VERSE TO LEARN
I will not forget (God's) word. (Psalm 119:16, *KJV*)

LET'S TALK TO GOD
Dear God, Jesus certainly must love us, to come to earth as a baby and grow up and have to LEARN just like anybody else. If he did all these things then he must understand EXACTLY how WE feel. That's a pretty wonderful thing to know when we get discouraged. Thank you a lot, Lord. In Jesus' name, Amen.

NOW FIND THIS STORY IN YOUR BIBLE
It's in Luke 2:40 and 46 and 47 and 52.

STORY 20

LOST: ONE BOY

Jesus could hardly wait until he was twelve years old. Because when he was twelve years old, something VERY IMPORTANT was going to happen. He was going to go with Mary and Joseph to the big Temple in Jerusalem! Every year, fathers and mothers traveled to the big Temple to worship—but boys couldn't go to the Temple services until they were twelve.

All his life, Jesus thought about the wonderful day when he would be allowed to go. And at last he was twelve!

Oh, joy! Such scrubbing and packing and cooking to get ready! What a golden day it was when Mary and Joseph and Jesus started out, with their little donkey packed right up to his long ears. What fun to meet other families along the way and travel along together. There were donkeys and camels and carts

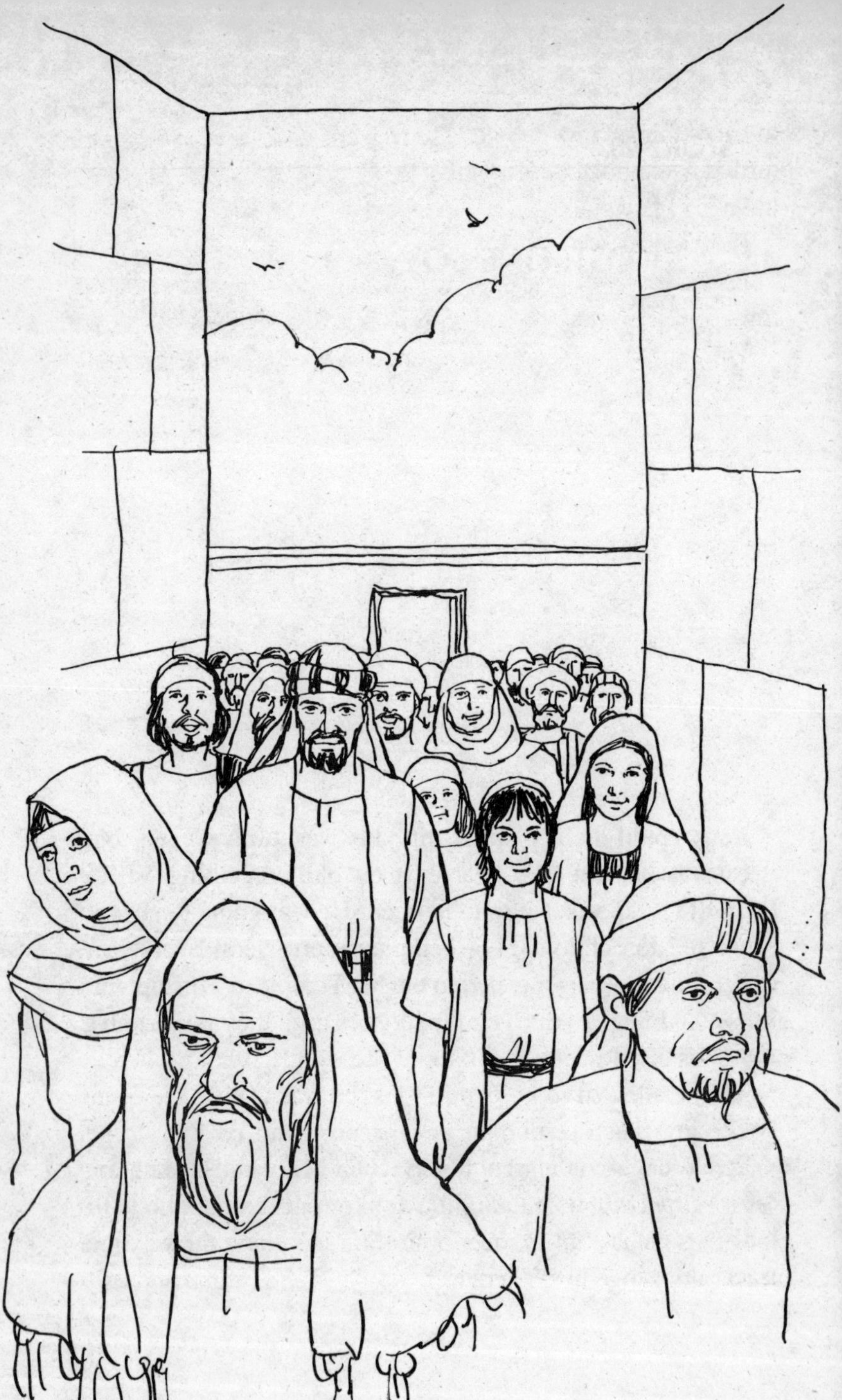

to carry things and people. There were goats and sheep and turtledoves and cattle to give to God. There were days of traveling. And finally—

JERUSALEM!

Jerusalem—with its funny, crooked cobblestone streets and rows of stores right outdoors. And the TEMPLE!

They could see its golden roof from a distance. They went through its big gates and into the huge courts. Of course, they could not go into the INNER courts. They could not see the rich curtains of red and blue and purple—and great chests made of brass—and candlesticks made of gold. But they went each day to worship God. And at last it was time to go back to Nazareth.

Mary and Joseph thought Jesus was with them when they started across the hills with the crowd. But when they stopped in the evening to rest, they looked for him—and he was GONE!

How dreadful! They went through the crowds, asking everybody. Nobody had seen him. Mary and Joseph went back to Jerusalem again, and for three days they looked in the streets, in the homes of their friends—everywhere. Then they looked in the Temple—

And there he was!

Not playing. Not crying. But sitting with the wise men of the Temple, talking about the things of God! Jesus was answering the questions of the wise men, and they were surprised at how much he knew.

"Why have you done this, my son?" Mary asked him. "We've been looking for you everywhere."

"You didn't look in the right place," said Jesus. "Didn't you know I'd be here about my Father's business?"

They went back home to Nazareth, and the days went on exactly as they had before.

But Jesus had given Mary and Joseph quite a jolt. He reminded them of WHO HE WAS. They never forgot that day, when Jesus was twelve years old. And they never forgot that Jesus is really God's own son.

LET'S TALK ABOUT THE BIBLE STORY

This was the first time Jesus ever acted as if he were really God's son. How do you suppose it made Mary and Joseph feel? What did the inside of the Temple look like? Do you know what his "Father's business" was? (See Story 9.) How do you think Jesus felt about God's house?

A BIBLE VERSE TO LEARN

I was glad when they said to me, "Let us go to the house of the LORD." (Psalm 122:1, *NASB*)

LET'S TALK TO GOD

Dear God, we thank you for sending Jesus to earth to die for us and rise again into heaven so we could be with him there some day. We thank you that you made him a baby and a boy and all the rest, because that helps us to understand him better, and we know he understands us and how we feel. In Jesus' name, Amen.

NOW FIND THIS STORY IN YOUR BIBLE

It's in Luke 2:40-52.

STORY 21

THE CHILDREN FIND A FRIEND

The day the wonderful news came, the little town by the lake was turned upside down with excitement, and nothing was ever quite the same again. The news was—well it was so exciting that it spread like wildfire!

The children heard it in the streets, and they ran into their houses, falling over pet lambs and sending pigeons flying in every direction.

"Mother! Jesus is here!"

And their mothers stopped mixing the bread dough and said, "Jesus? Where?"

"Here, Mother, HERE. He's on his way to Jerusalem, and

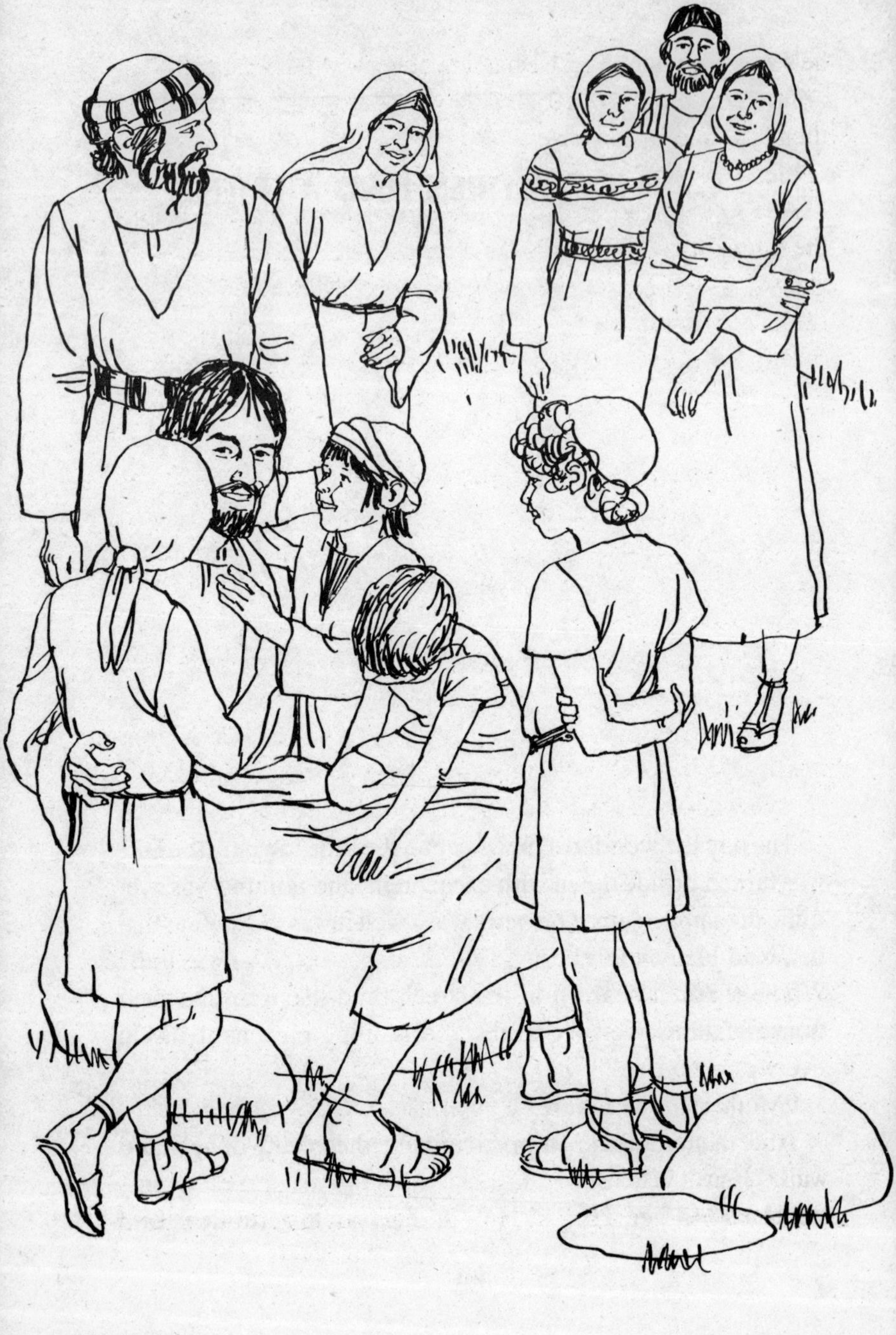

he's stopping here and he has his helpers with him, and—"

But their mothers had already rinsed their hands and dried them on their aprons.

"Jesus is here!" they cried. "Go get your father!"

And so the news spread, until everybody knew about it, and the fishing was forgotten and the shops were closed. Everybody wanted to see Jesus. The mothers especially wanted Jesus to bless their children.

Perhaps if they hurried and got there early, they could see him. The children stuck close to their mothers, and they all talked at once as they hurried to the place where Jesus was.

But when they got there, the most DREADFUL of all things happened. They couldn't even get near him!

The mothers tried to get through the crowd. The children tried to squiggle through. But they couldn't.

The mothers thought perhaps if they spoke to Jesus' disciples, THEN they could see him. "Please—" they began, "We wondered if perhaps—"

"What do you want here?" the disciples said. Well, that wasn't a very good beginning. But the mothers grew bolder.

"We want Jesus to bless our children!" they cried. And the disciples said, "Go away. Jesus isn't interested in children."

Well. That was that. The mothers and children turned sadly away. It was no use. But then—That WASN'T that!

"Don't turn the children away," said a voice. Who was that? Who was THAT? They listened hard. "Bring them here to me," the voice went on. It was JESUS! Oh, joy!

Could it be true?

It WAS! The crowd was separating to let them through!

The children started to walk toward Jesus, slowly. Then they walked faster. Then they RAN. They ran right up to him and stood around him, by his knee—and he put his hand on their heads and blessed them. Oh, it was wonderful. It was better than they had dared dream!

They all went home happy. And on evenings when they sat in their doorways, they had something to talk about for years.

The little town was never quite the same again. Jesus had stopped there.

The fathers and mothers were never quite the same again. For they had SEEN him.

And the children were never quite the same again. For they had TOUCHED him!

LET'S TALK ABOUT THE BIBLE STORY

Do you think Jesus cares just as much about children today? What are some things in your life that make you think that Jesus cares about you? What has God given you to READ so you'll know Jesus cares about you personally?

A BIBLE VERSE TO LEARN

We love (God), because he first loved us. (1 John 4:19, *KJV*)

LET'S TALK TO GOD

Dear God, you have loved us for a long long time, even before we knew you. And you love us today. You tell us so in the Bible. And you let us know by all the things you do for us. We thank you for your great love. Help us to love you back even better than ever before. In Jesus' name, Amen.

NOW FIND THIS STORY IN YOUR BIBLE

It's in Matthew 19:13-15 and Mark 10:13-16 and Luke 18:15-17.

STORY 22

THE BOY THE DOCTORS COULDN'T CURE

The beautiful house in Capernaum was quiet. The nobleman who lived there was brokenhearted. His little boy was very, very sick.

"There is nothing we can do for him," said the doctors. And they shook their heads.

"Nothing to do—nothing to do—" thought the nobleman, as he stood by his son's bed. "Nothing, unless—"

Then he suddenly thought of something! Jesus was in the town of Cana! The nobleman had heard his friends telling wonderful tales of how Jesus was teaching, and curing the sick—

"Get my horse ready," the nobleman said to his servants. "I'm going to Cana!"

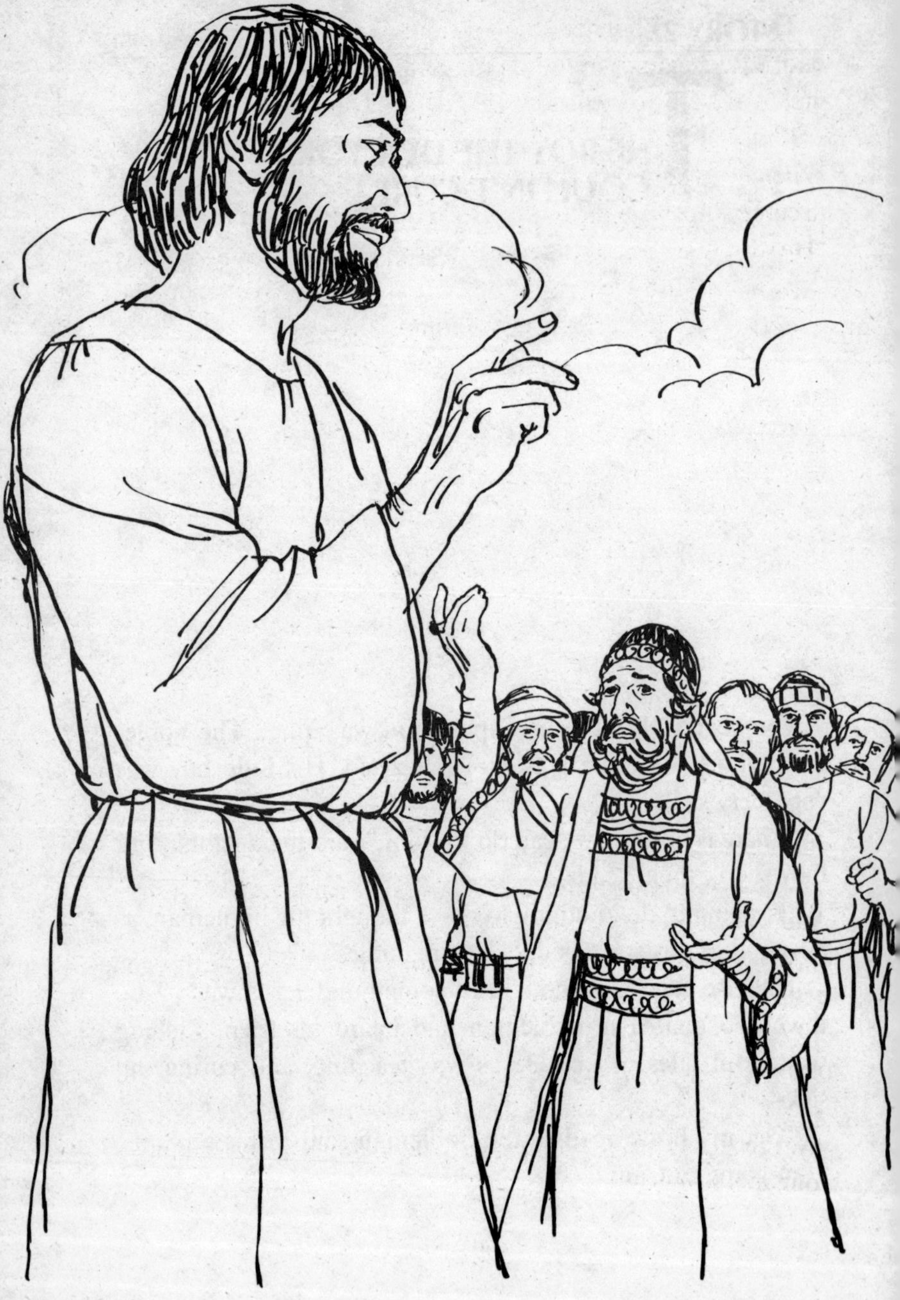

The servants hurried to obey, and as the nobleman left, he said, "Take care of my son. I'm going to bring Jesus back with me!" And off he went to Cana as fast as he could go.

It was about one o'clock when the nobleman got to Cana. When he saw the crowds, his heart sank. "Jesus will be too busy to come," he thought, as he pushed his way through the crowd. "He won't be able to come, and my son will die," he thought, as he struggled to get up close to where Jesus was. By the time he got to Jesus, the nobleman was almost crying.

"Please, Jesus!" he said. "Come to Capernaum and heal my son!"

Jesus looked at the nobleman, with the kindest eyes in the world. Jesus didn't say he would come. He didn't say he WOULDN'T come. He said something far more wonderful. He simply said, "Go back home. Your son is well."

And suddenly, in his heart, the nobleman KNEW that his son was well. He thanked Jesus, and went back through the crowds, and started for home. All his fear was gone. He knew Jesus meant what he said.

All the way home he thought about it. And as he got near his house—

Servants from his house—running to meet him! "Your son did not die!" they cried. "He is well!"

"I know—I know!" said the nobleman. "Jesus healed him!" And they all started back for the house.

"Just when," asked the nobleman, "did my son start to get better?"

"About one o'clock," they cried. "Yes—it was just one o'clock."

"Ahhh," he said quietly, "that is just what I expected you to say. For that is just the hour Jesus said to me, 'Go back home—your son is well.'"

And they bowed their heads then and there and thanked God.

And oh—the house in Capernaum was bright again! And the nobleman was happy. Jesus had healed his son without even seeing him. Nobody else could do that.

But Jesus could. He is the son of God.

LET'S TALK ABOUT THE BIBLE STORY

Actually we have doctors to help make us well. But who do you suppose helps the doctors? Do you think it's right to ask God to make us better when we have doctors? Why?

A BIBLE VERSE TO LEARN

(Jesus) healed many that were sick. (Mark 1:34, *KJV*)

LET'S TALK TO GOD

Dear God, we thank you that you care about us when we're sick. And we know that you can help the doctors make us better, and sometimes you even help us when the doctors CAN'T. We love you. In Jesus' name, Amen.

NOW FIND THIS STORY IN YOUR BIBLE

It's in John 4:46-53.

STORY 23

THE MAN WHO COULDN'T SEE

Jeffrey and his friends are playing Blind Man's Bluff, and Jeffrey is "it." How strange everything is behind that dark bandage! Jeffrey can't see a thing and he can't tell WHICH way he is going. The other children are supposed to keep quiet so he won't know where they are, but he has just bumped into a chair and it was so FUNNY they laughed before they remembered. Such fun! But Jeffrey is "blind" for only a few minutes. If he were REALLY blind all the time—it wouldn't be funny at all.

Bartimaeus was blind, and there wasn't a chance in the world that he would ever see. He lived in Jericho, but he never saw the gardens and palm trees and market places. He sat by the side of the street and begged for money, but he never saw the crowds that went by or the people who stopped to give him

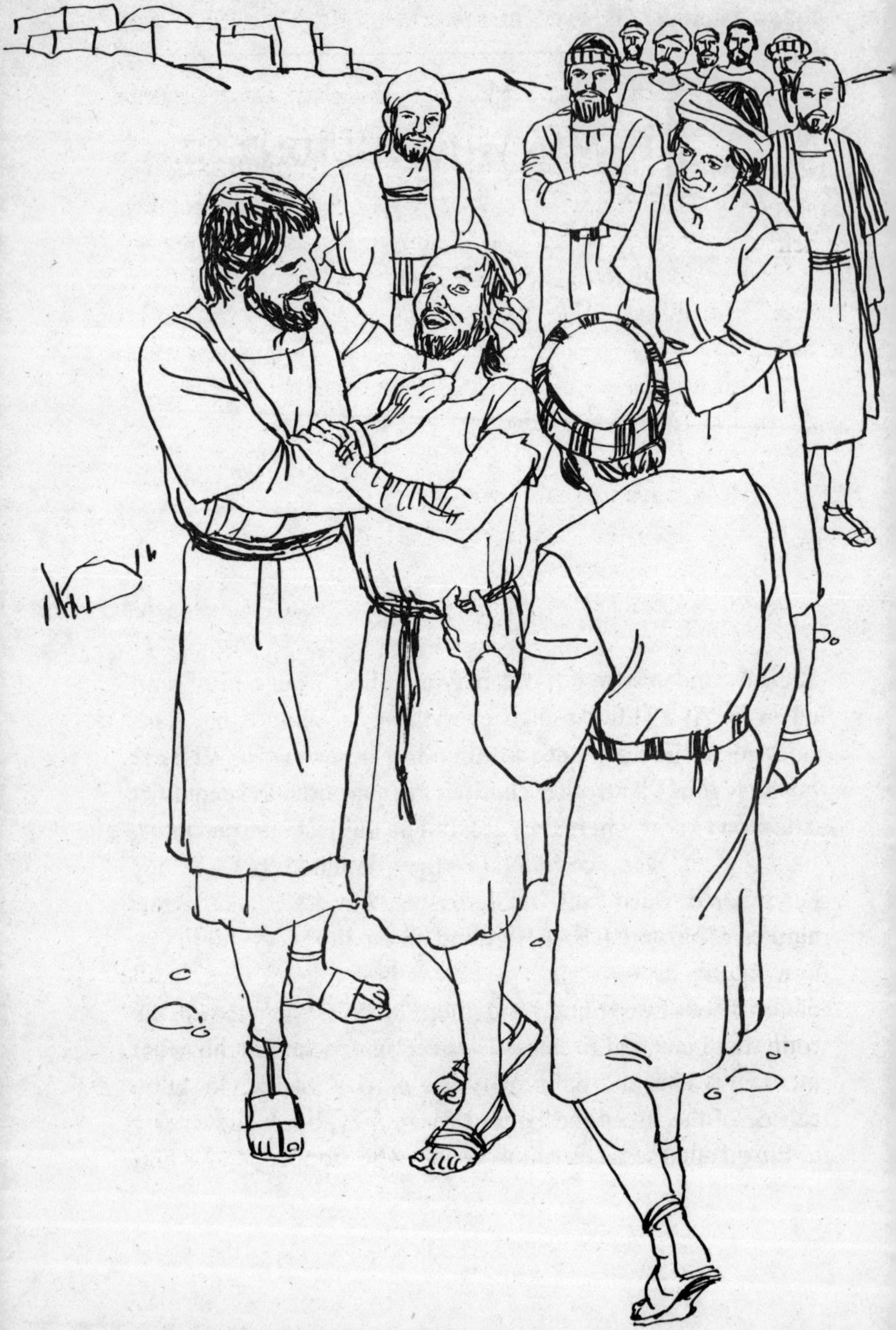

a few pennies. He lived in a world of BLACKNESS. And nobody seemed to care.

One day, Bartimaeus felt his way along the streets until he came to the big city gate. He sat down against the wall and began to beg. The people hurried by. He heard the clop-clop of the donkeys. Some sheep passed by so close he could touch their woolly sides. It was just like any other day. And then—

There was a sudden excitement in the air. He could FEEL it. People scrambled off to the side of the road. They backed up until they crowded against him. Everybody was talking at once.

"What is it?" cried Bartimaeus. "What's going on?" And he listened HARD to the voices around him.

"It's Jesus!"

"He's on his way to Jerusalem!"

"Out of the way, there. Back up!"

"There he is now!"

Oh, yes—Jesus. Bartimaeus could understand the excitement. No wonder! People followed Jesus everywhere. He taught them, and healed them—

He HEALED them—

Suddenly Bartimaeus' heart did a flip-flop. A great wild hope zoomed up inside of him. "Jesus—have mercy on me!" he shouted.

"Be quiet!" the people told him. "Stop shouting."

But Bartimaeus didn't stop. "Jesus—help me!" he cried, and he scrambled to his feet. And then—

Everyone grew quiet. Jesus had stopped, right in the middle of the road. He said something to his disciples. Bartimaeus could hear people mumbling. Then he could feel them jostling, moving sideways. He listened HARD. And then someone called, "Jesus wants to talk to you."

Bartimaeus could hardly believe it! He threw off his coat and he started to move forward. Then somebody took his arm. And the next thing he knew—

"What is it you want me to do for you?" It was the kindest voice. It was Jesus!

"Lord, that I might receive my sight!" said Bartimaeus through the blackness. And then—Jesus spoke softly—

"Because you believe that I can do this for you, you shall see."

The blackness rolled away like a cloud. And there before Bartimaeus' eyes—stood Jesus! Bartimaeus could SEE him. And all around him—
> men and women
>   and bright-colored robes
>   and the city gates—

oh, so many things, Bartimaeus didn't know where to look first! It was a great ocean of color! Then he looked back at Jesus. He said "thank you" to Jesus in every way he could think of. And when Jesus turned to walk down the road, Bartimaeus followed along with the crowd. He forgot how he had planned to spend the day. He forgot EVERYTHING—except that he loved Jesus—and that he could SEE.

Bartimaeus had been blind. And there wasn't a chance in the world that he would ever see—until Jesus came along. Now he could see everything—like an ocean of color. But best of all—he could see JESUS.

LET'S TALK ABOUT THE BIBLE STORY

Think of some of the wonderful things you see every day. Can you name a few of them? And how about all the things you learn. Could you learn as fast if you couldn't see? And what if you couldn't see your friends? Would you like them as much? But supposing you really COULDN'T see.

A BIBLE VERSE TO LEARN

Jesus of Nazareth . . . went about doing good. (Acts 10:38, KJV)

LET'S TALK TO GOD

Dear God, we certainly do thank you for all the beautiful things we can see around us. (Thank him for some of the special things you can see.)

NOW FIND THIS STORY IN YOUR BIBLE

It's in Mark 10:46-52 and Luke 18:35-43.

STORY 24

THE MOST EXTRAORDINARY LUNCH IN THE WORLD

Back in the land where Jesus lived, an ordinary boy started off on an ordinary hike, on an ordinary day. He didn't know it, but it was going to be the most important day in his life! His mother gave him an ordinary lunch. Oh, it was a VERY ordinary lunch. Five barley loaves and two little dried fishes!

He whistled along the hills and up and down the paths. He whistled his way clear down to the shores of Lake Galilee.

Then he stopped.

There was a bigger crowd of people than he had ever seen before—more than five thousand people! They weren't standing. They seemed to be GOING someplace. And being filled with an ordinary amount of curiosity, he asked where they were going.

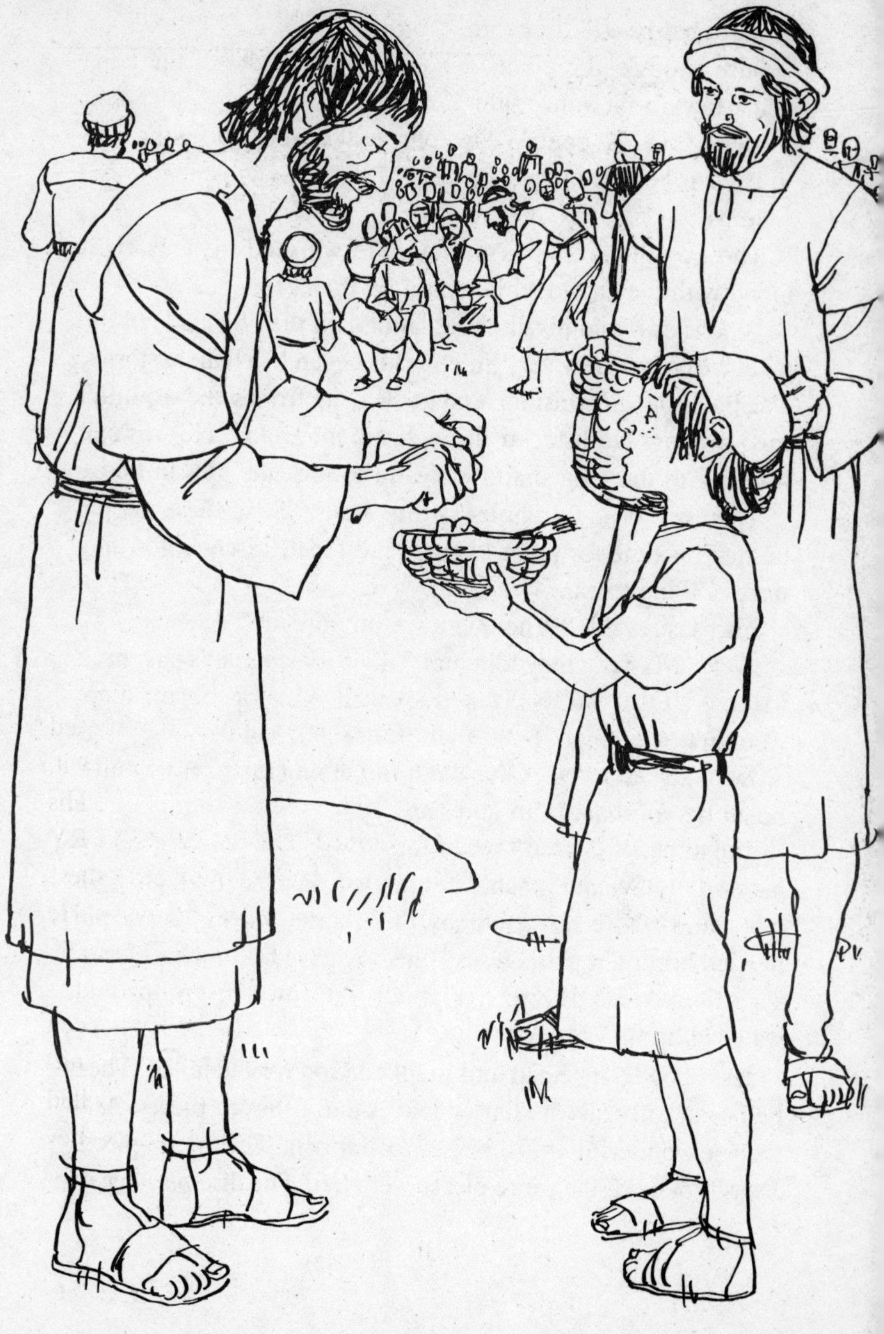

"See that boat?" they said.

Sure enough, there was a boat in the middle of the lake, going toward the other side.

"Jesus is in that boat. We're going to the other side of the lake so we can be there when he lands!"

Jesus!

The boy didn't stop a minute. He whistled his way right along with the crowd so he could be there, too.

When Jesus and his disciples landed on the other side of the lake, the crowd grew very quiet. Jesus began to tell them stories. The boy stopped whistling and got way up front so he wouldn't miss a thing. He listened through the afternoon. He was still listening as the long shadows began to tuck the hills in bed.

Then one of the disciples said to Jesus, "Send these people home. It is time for them to get bread for themselves, for they have nothing to eat."

And Jesus said, "Where can we buy bread?"

"Why, Master," they told him, "if we took a man's paycheck for a WHOLE MONTH and spent it ALL on bread, there wouldn't be enough. Send them home."

But Jesus said, "No. Give them something to eat. How much bread do you have? Go and see."

The disciples started toward the crowd. The boy pricked up his ears. "I have my lunch!" he shouted. Just like that. He held it up—and before you could say, "five barley loaves," a disciple had led him right up to Jesus! The boy gave his lunch to Jesus. Then he watched hard. Everybody sat down in groups and watched hard.

Jesus bowed his head and thanked God for the lunch. Then he began to break the barley loaves and fishes in pieces. And then a wonderful thing began to happen. The more pieces Jesus broke off, the more pieces were left! The disciples began to pass them out, walking between the groups of people. And when the disciples came back, there were MORE pieces. There were just pieces and pieces and PIECES. Even after everyone was fed there was enough left to fill—twelve baskets!

The boy looked at what was left over from his ordinary lunch. It was hard to believe. He had started out on an ordinary hike on an ordinary day. It had started out just like any other day. But it turned out to be the most important day of his life.

Nothing was very ORDINARY when Jesus was around!

LET'S TALK ABOUT THE BIBLE STORY

Just imagine sitting on a hillside listening to JESUS tell stories! What are some things Jesus might have taught the people about God? How do you suppose the boy felt about sharing his lunch? What do you think he thought about before he shouted out that he had something to share? How do you suppose it made him feel after he saw what Jesus did with it?

A BIBLE VERSE TO LEARN

Give us this day our daily bread. (Matthew 6:11, *KJV*)

LET'S TALK TO GOD

Dear God, thank you for letting our food grow in the ground so farmers can gather it and markets can get it and our mothers and fathers can buy it. We know that all food, no matter how we get it, is from YOU in the first place. Help us to share whenever we have a chance and not be stingy and keep everything to ourselves. In Jesus' name, Amen.

NOW FIND THIS STORY IN YOUR BIBLE

It's in Matthew 14:13-21 and Mark 6:32-44 and Luke 9:10-17 and John 6:1-14.

STORY 25

THE MAN WHO WENT THROUGH THE ROOF

The poor man had been sick for years and years. There wasn't a doctor in the world who could heal him. He couldn't even move. Other people had to care for him. Every day was just like every other day. Nothing ever happened.

And then—
    one day—
the whole town was all astir. Up one street and down another, people were passing the word along. Jesus was in town!

The friends of the sick man thought, "How wonderful it would be if Jesus would make this poor man well." Then they got busy.

They tied a rope to each corner of his mat-bed so they could carry him. They—hup!—lifted him up and started off to find Jesus. And then they ran into—

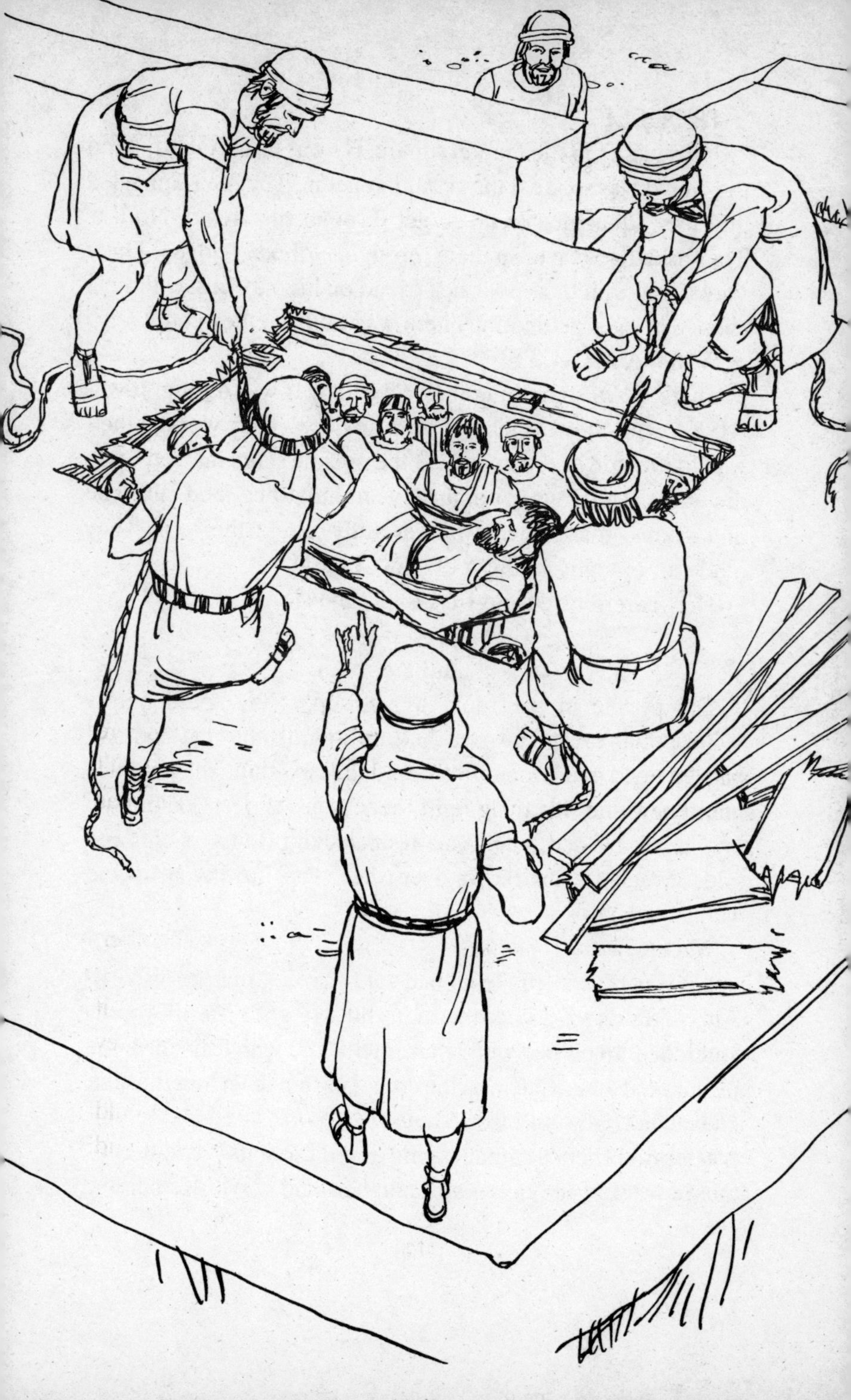

TROUBLE.

Jesus wasn't in the market square. He was in a HOUSE—and the crowd was so great they couldn't get in. The men squiggled and they squaggled to try to get through the crowd. No use. They asked people to let them through. Nobody budged. There they stood, with their poor sick friend on his mat-bed, without a chance of ever getting in. There was nothing they could—

WAIT A MINUTE!

There WAS something they could do! It was daring. It was RISKY. But they decided to do it anyhow. They worked their way to the side of the house—to the outside stairs that led up to the roof. And—hup!—up they went, mat-bed and all. The men—oops—made their way carefully across the roof. They made an opening in the roof—and THEN—

They carefully, c-a-r-e-f-u-l-l-y let the sick man
down—d-o-w-n
into the room.

The people in the room looked up. They could hardly believe their eyes! They reached up to grab the mat-bed and backed up to make room for it. And the next thing the poor sick man knew—he was lying right there at Jesus' feet, looking up into Jesus' blessed face! And Jesus looked down at him and said, "Son, thy sins be forgiven thee. Pick up thy bed—and walk."

WALK!

Everybody waited. Jesus had told the sick man to WALK! And that's exactly what the man did. He got up with wonder and rolled up his bed with amazement, and with tear-filled eyes he thanked Jesus. Then, as the crowd parted to let him through, he walked right out of that house.

His good friends came leaping down the stairs. And they all met in front of the house and laughed and cried together and probably even hugged each other! How wonderful it was! It was almost too good to be true!

The sick man was now well and oh so happy. Because Jesus, the Son of God, healed him. And because he had friends who CARED enough to BRING him to Jesus!

LET'S TALK ABOUT THE BIBLE STORY

Is there any way you can think of that the sick man could have got to Jesus without his friends? Was there any time along the way that they could have given up? Aren't you glad they didn't? Can you think of any friends who have gone out of their way to take you to Sunday School or Bible School? Have you gone out of your way to take anyone else to where they could learn about Jesus?

A BIBLE VERSE TO LEARN

Through love serve one another. (Galatians 5:13, *NASB*)

LET'S TALK TO GOD

Dear God, we thank you for every friend we have who cares about us. Help us to be willing to go out of our way to take our friends where they can hear about Jesus. In Jesus' name, Amen.

NOW FIND THIS STORY IN YOUR BIBLE

It's in Mark 2:1-12 and Luke 5:17-26.

STORY 26
THE DAY JESUS DIDN'T HURRY

The only one who could help Jairus—was Jesus.

"Hurry, hurry, hurry," thought Jairus, as he left his house. "Hurry, hurry, hurry," he thought as he went through the streets to the lakeside. He HAD to find Jesus. And for a very important reason. His daughter was very, very sick—and if he didn't hurry, she would die.

When Jairus got to the lakeside, the crowd was so great, his heart nearly stopped beating. Would he be on time? Would Jesus come? "Hurry, hurry, hurry," he thought, as he squeezed his way through the crowd.

Then—at last—there was Jesus!

Jairus ran up to him and fell down at his feet and said, "Oh Jesus—my little girl is so sick she is going to die. Please come and make her well!"

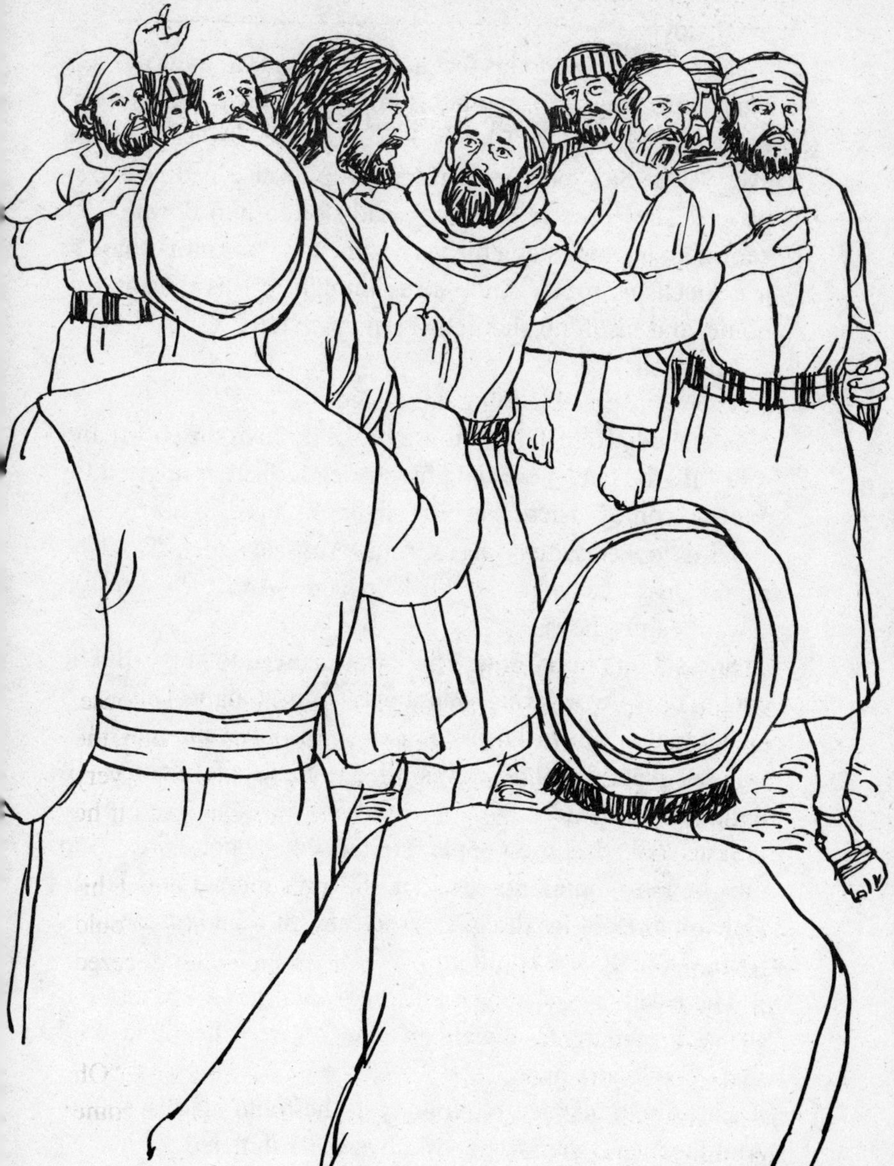

And Jesus said, "Yes, I will go with you."

Oh, joy!

Jairus scrambled to his feet and began to lead the way. "Oh hurry, hurry, hurry," sang in his mind. But the crowds were so great, they COULDN'T hurry. People pressed in on Jesus from every side. Sick people—curious people—nice people—noisy people. They pressed him back and slowed him down. They kept stopping him along the way, some to talk to him—some to just touch his robes. And Jairus thought of his daughter at home, and his mind shouted—"Hurry—HURRY!"

And then—

The worst possible thing happened.

Somebody from Jairus' house broke through the crowd and said, "It's too late! Your daughter is dead. There is no need for Jesus to come." There was no longer any need to hurry.

Jairus looked sadly at Jesus. And Jesus said softly, "Don't be afraid. Just trust me—and I'll help you." And they went on toward Jairus' house.

Jairus didn't hurry now. There was no need to hurry. But he couldn't help wondering. What was Jesus going to DO?

When they got to Jairus' house—Jairus knew the news was true, all right. The house was filled with people—crying. His daughter was dead.

Jesus looked at the people. He looked at poor Jairus. And then he took command. He took the girl's mother and Jairus. He took three of his disciples. And they all went into the girl's room. Nobody else could go in.

There was the girl lying on the bed—and she looked just as if she were sleeping. Jesus went up to her and took her hand—and said—"Little girl, arise."

Jairus held his breath. Nobody in the room made a sound. And then—and then—The girl's eyelashes fluttered.

She began to breathe.

She sat up and looked around.

Then she STOOD UP!

There she was, standing before them—alive, and completely well again!

The only one who could have helped her—was Jesus. And it didn't matter whether he hurried or not. Jesus could do anything. He is the Son of God.

LET'S TALK ABOUT THE BIBLE STORY

Why do you suppose Jesus made Jairus wait? What do you think that taught Jairus? Can you think of times when your mother and dad have told you that you would have to wait for something you wanted very badly? What were the reasons you had to wait? Can you think of times when God has answered your prayers by saying, "Wait. I will give you this at a better time?" Aren't you glad God always answers your prayers in the way he knows is best?

A BIBLE VERSE TO LEARN

Jesus said, *"Don't be afraid. Just trust me."* (Mark 5:36, *TLB*)

LET'S TALK TO GOD

Dear God, help us to be willing to wait and not be in such a hurry every time we want something. Thank you for caring when we're sick. Thank you for our mothers and fathers who care for us when we're sick and when we're well too. And thank you for answering our prayers in the way you know is best. In Jesus' name, Amen.

NOW FIND THIS STORY IN YOUR BIBLE

It's in Mark 5:21-43 and Luke 8:40-56.

STORY 27

AN EXCITING DAY IN JERUSALEM (PALM SUNDAY)

The disciples had no way of knowing what an exciting day this was going to be. It started out just like any other trip.

They left the little village where they had been staying, early in the morning. It was ordinary enough. Just Jesus and his disciples. As they walked along the road, people began to join them. The day was quiet and bright and blue. The disciples could hardly notice the excitement at first. They could just sort of FEEL it beginning.

It began when Jesus asked two of his disciples to go ahead to the next village and get a donkey. "Not just ANY donkey," he told them. "There's a CERTAIN donkey. Untie him and bring him to me."

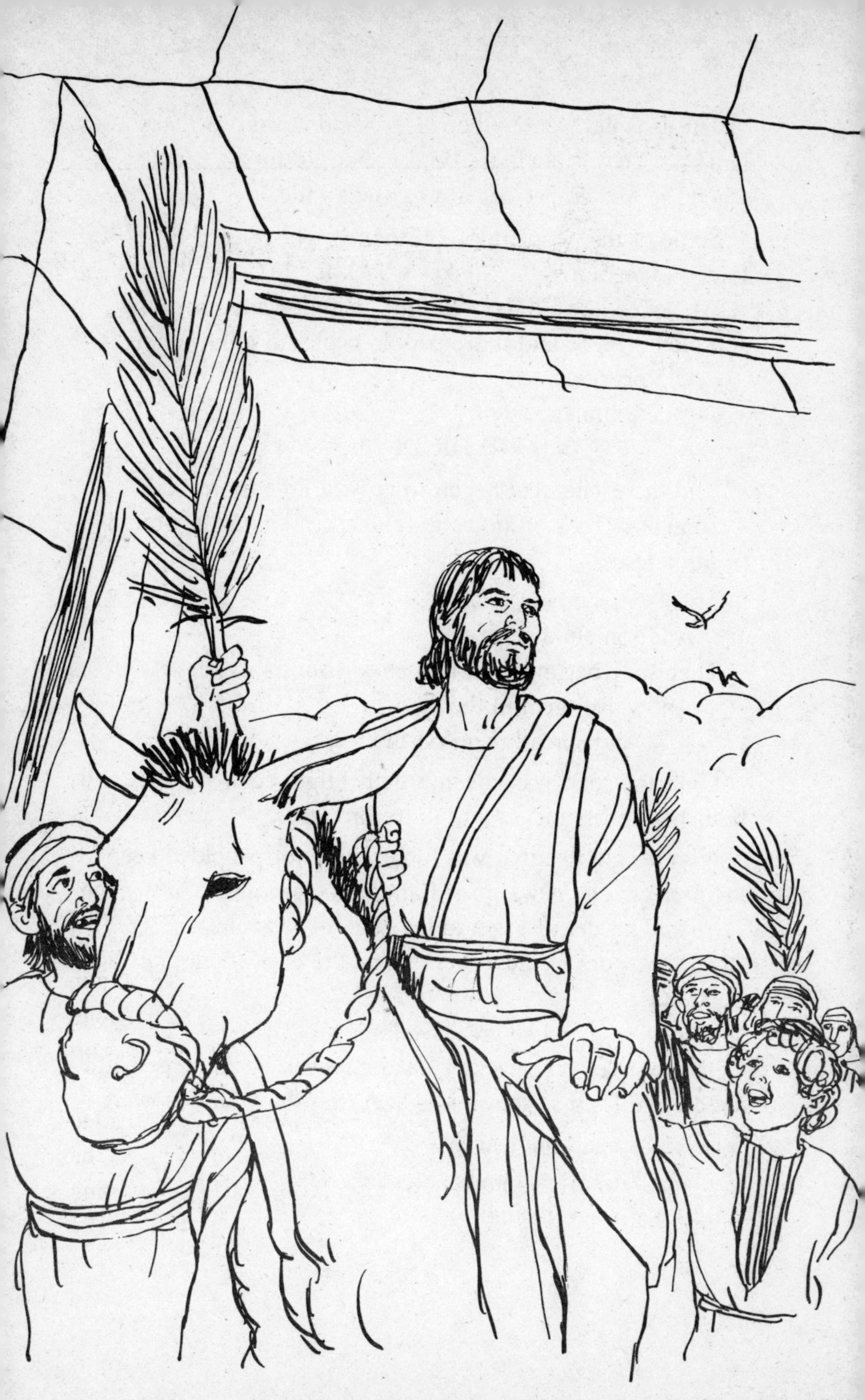

The disciples went to the village—and it was exactly as Jesus had said. They brought the donkey back to Jesus—and that was when the excitement began to grow a little.

Some of the people took off their bright-colored robes and folded them across the donkey's back for Jesus to sit on. Now Jesus looked like a KING, as they went down the road toward Jerusalem. More and more people began to follow along.

    Old people.

        Young people.

            And CHILDREN.

And the excitement began to grow a little more.

Somebody took off his robe—and spread it on the ground in front of Jesus.

    Then somebody else did.

    And somebody else.

Then they began to cut branches from palm trees.

    And wave them in the air.

    And spread them on the road.

Until the road was covered with bright-colored robes and branches and branches and more branches.

Now a sight like that was too exciting for people to keep to themselves. The news spread ahead to Jerusalem. And when Jesus and his disciples got to the gates of Jerusalem—EVERYBODY was out to meet them! And the excitement grew and burst out—

        like great swelling MUSIC.

The people were packed on both sides of the streets—the children in front so they could see. And they threw flowers.

    And spread out leaves.

        And waved palm branches

            And sang!

They sang, "Hosanna in the highest. Blessed is he that comes in the name of the Lord!"

And from the city gates to the great Temple with the golden roof—that song was in the air. The children sang it in the streets. They sang it in the Temple courts. They filled the air with it. It was one of the most exciting days they'd ever had in Jerusalem. The old people
>and young people
>>and children

all wanted Jesus to know how much they loved him!

And they TOLD him so!

LET'S TALK ABOUT THE BIBLE STORY

Can you think of all the different ways you can praise God in Sunday School? In church? Can you name some ways you can praise him during the week?

A BIBLE VERSE TO LEARN

Sing to the Lord with thanksgiving. (Psalm 147:7, *NASB*)

LET'S TALK TO GOD

Dear God, we ARE thankful for you. You are so good to us! Help us to behave in ways that are pleasing to you every day in the week. We know that this is one way we can praise you. In Jesus' name, Amen.

NOW FIND THIS STORY IN YOUR BIBLE

It's in Matthew 21:1-11 and Mark 11:1-10 and Luke 19:29-38.

STORY 28

THE SADDEST DAY (GOOD FRIDAY)

Oh, that was a glad day, when Jesus rode into Jerusalem on the donkey and people spread their robes and waved palm branches and the children sang and sang until the music seemed to rise to the very skies! It seemed absolutely impossible that anything dreadful could happen after such a glad day.

But it did.

It all began with some people who did not believe that Jesus is the son of God. It would have been quite dreadful enough if they just didn't believe it, and let it go at that. But they didn't stop there. They sent a band of soldiers after him. And the soldiers caught him in a garden where he was praying to God. And they arrested him and dragged him before the ruler. And the ruler had him tied to a post and whipped. It would have been dreadful enough if they had stopped THERE. But they did not.

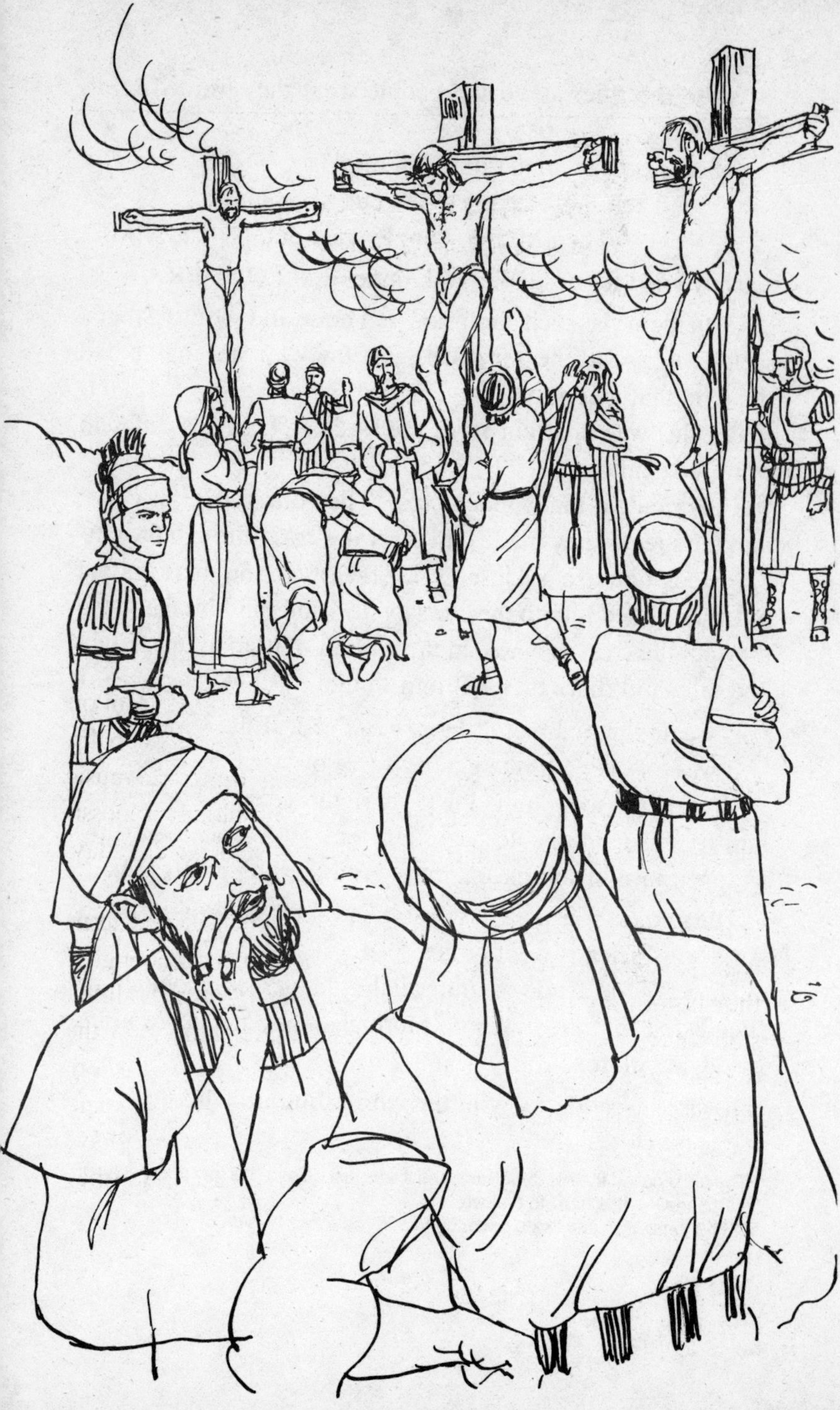

When the ruler asked the people what they wanted to do with Jesus—

Some people cried out, "Kill him!"

Then more people cried out, "Kill him!"

Then MORE people cried out, "KILL HIM!"

They cried it out louder and louder and LOUDER.

Until there was such confusion and noise and shouting that it seemed to rise to the very skies, just the way the singing had done on that glad day!

But this was different from the singing. This was different from the glad day.

They made a big wooden cross. They dragged Jesus down into the street. They made him carry the cross through the city. They took him to a hill just outside the city.* And there on that hill, they nailed him to the cross by his hands and his feet. And they put the cross in a hole in the ground so it stood up straight and tall. And there they left him to die.

It seemed incredible!** Jesus was dead. JESUS was dead!

It was all over. All the gladness was over.

His friends took him down from the cross. They carried him—oh so tenderly—to a garden tomb.*** And there they wrapped him in soft clean cloths. And there they left him.

The soldiers rolled a HUGE stone over the door of the tomb. And Jesus' friends went home.

He was gone. And with him, all the gladness was gone. Jesus' friends felt that there was no more gladness, anywhere in the world, anymore.

It was the saddest day in the world. But little did they

---

* The hill is called the hill of Calvary, and it was just outside the city of Jerusalem.
** This means it is hard to believe.
***The tomb was just like a cave, carved in the rocky hillside.

know—there was a GLAD day coming! Just around the corner! The GLADDEST day in the world!

LET'S TALK ABOUT THE BIBLE STORY
Everything seems to be in a hopeless state. But do you remember way back when Adam and Eve disobeyed God and "spoiled it all?" (See Genesis 3:1-24.) Why, Jesus left his home in heaven and came to earth to die on the cross because he LOVES you! This is what the Bible means when it says that Jesus Christ came to be your Saviour. Believe it! Let him KNOW you believe it! It's the most wonderful news in the world!

A BIBLE VERSE TO LEARN
God so loved the world (that means you), *that he gave his . . . Son, that whosoever* (that means you again) *BELIEVES in him shall . . . have everlasting life.* (John 3:16, *KJV*)

LET'S TALK TO GOD
Dear God, we know that from the beginning of the world you planned to have Jesus die for us. And when the time came, it happened, just as you planned it. We thank Jesus for doing this. And we thank YOU for loving us so much that you sent us a Saviour. In Jesus' name, Amen.

NOW FIND THIS STORY IN YOUR BIBLE
It's in Mark 15:1-47 and Luke 23:33-53.

STORY 29

THE GLADDEST DAY (EASTER)

The day started out to be sad. It was still the saddest time in the world for Jesus' friends. Some of them were SO sad that they got up early in the morning and hurried back to the tomb in the garden where they had left him—the tomb with the stone rolled in front of it. They knew it was all over and he was dead. But they had spices and sweet perfumes for him, and they hoped they'd find someone to roll the stone away.

They hurried to the garden, and actually that's all they expected to see—a tomb with a huge stone rolled over the doorway. But when they got there—

The great stone door of the tomb had been rolled away! And Jesus was GONE!

At first they just stood there, STUNNED.

And then they all did different things.

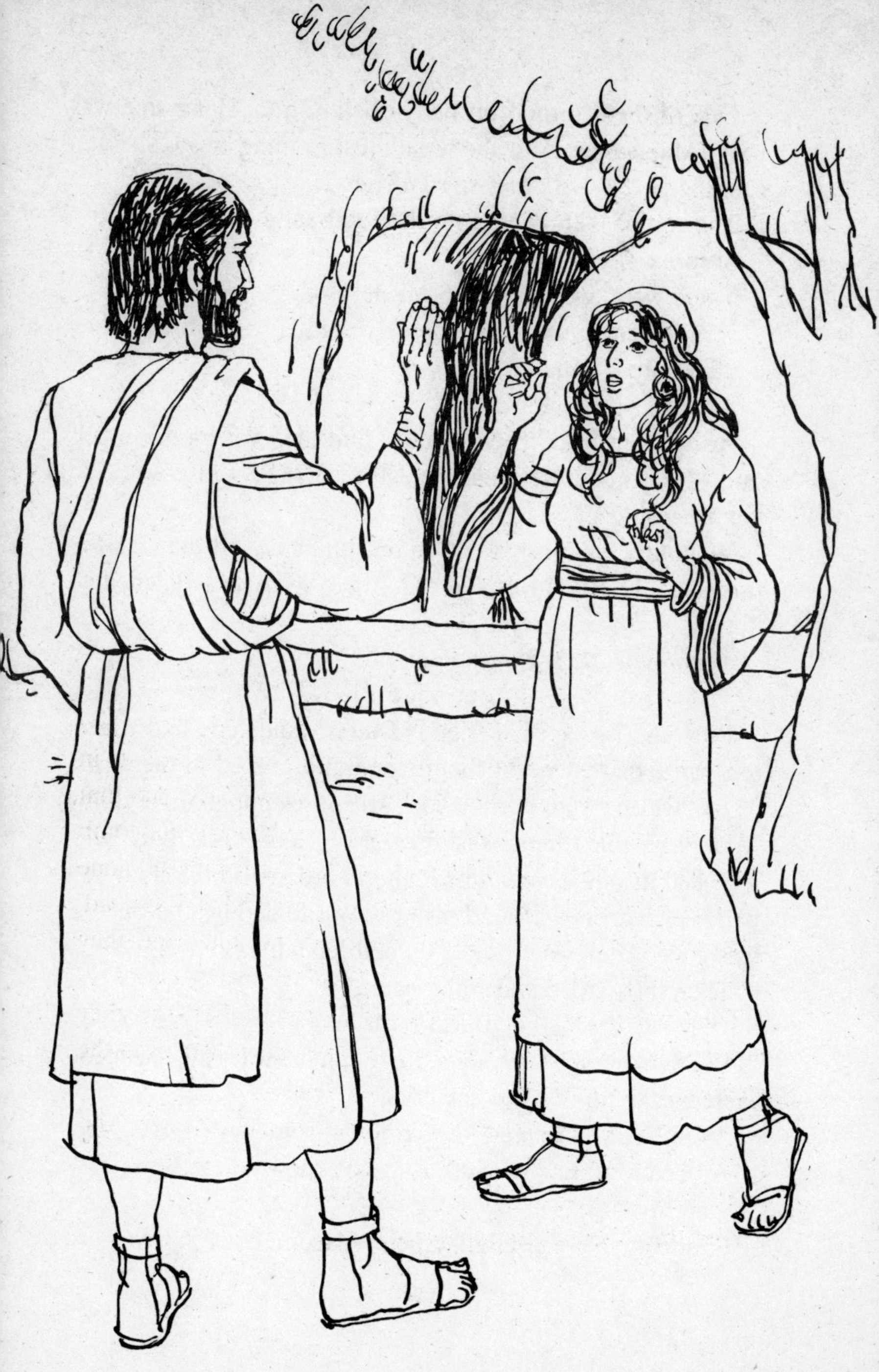

One of them turned on her heels and ran. Her name was Mary Magdalene. And she wasn't just running away. She was running to tell two other special friends.

The rest of them went into the tomb, and—

Surprise of all surprises!

There were two ANGELS inside!

Jesus' friends just stood there, absolutely speechless. They couldn't say a thing.

ANGELS!

And before Jesus' friends could find their voices, the angels said, "He is not dead. He is alive. He is RISEN—just as he told you he would be."

Well, first they just stood there, stunned. And then THEY turned on THEIR heels and ran, just as Mary Magdalene had done.

Then the garden was quiet.

But not for long.

First, the two special friends Mary Magdalene had run to tell, came back. One of them stood and looked in the tomb. The other one went right inside. And sure enough. Everything Mary had told them was true. The cloth Jesus had been wrapped in was there, all neat and in order, and the cloth that had been wrapped around his head was folded neatly. But HE was gone. They went out of the garden, amazed.

Then the garden was quiet again.

But not for long.

For last of all, Mary Magdalene came back. And she stood there by the tomb. And she cried.

"Why are you crying?" asked the angels.

And Mary said, "Because I do not know where Jesus is."

And then—

Suddenly she realized that there was somebody standing just

behind her. She turned around. It was a man, but in the early morning half-darkness she did not know him. She thought perhaps he might be the gardener.

"Why are you crying?" he asked. "And who are you looking for?"

"Oh," said Mary, "I'm looking for Jesus. Do YOU know where they have taken him?"

And the stranger said softly—oh so softly and lovingly—"Mary." Just like that.

And the MINUTE he said her name—"Mary"—she knew who he was.

It was JESUS! He was alive! Oh, joy!

"Jesus!" said Mary. It couldn't be true. But it WAS. He was standing right there. He was looking at her. And he SPOKE to her again.

"Go tell my friends that I'm alive," he said, "and that I'm going to heaven—just as I said I would."

And she did!

Oh, it was a GLAD day after all! It was a GLAD day! It was the GLADDEST day in the world!

Do you know what?

It was the first EASTER SUNDAY!

LET'S TALK ABOUT THE BIBLE STORY

Jesus is alive today—the BIBLE tells us so. He is with us, in our hearts. How can we talk to him? How can we listen to him speaking to us? Can you think of some of the many ways he helps you in your own life?

A BIBLE VERSE TO LEARN

Jesus said, *"I am with you always, even to the end of the world."* (Matthew 28:20, *TLB*)

Another verse to learn:
I am alive for evermore. (Revelation 1:18, *KJV*)

LET'S TALK TO GOD

Dear God, how we thank you that when we sing the song, "Jesus loves me, this I know, for the Bible tells me so," it isn't just a lot of WORDS. The Bible DOES tell us so, and it's all true. How wonderful it is that Jesus is alive and we can talk to each other. We appreciate this, God. And we thank you. In Jesus' name, Amen.

NOW FIND THIS STORY IN YOUR BIBLE

It's in Matthew 28:1-20 and Mark 16:1-15 and Luke 24:1-12.

STORY 30

THE BEST NEWS! (ASCENSION)

Yes, Easter was the gladdest day in the world. Jesus had come out of the tomb alive. Mary had seen him. And she had run to tell all his friends, just as he had asked her to.

And after that they saw him—not every day as they used to—but at the most surprising times!

One time two of them were just walking along the road on their way to a town called Emmaus—and there he was—walking along the road!

One time some of them just got back from fishing all night—and there he was—on the shore!

One time some of them were gathered together in a room in Jerusalem—and there he was—right in the room!

And then, ONE time—

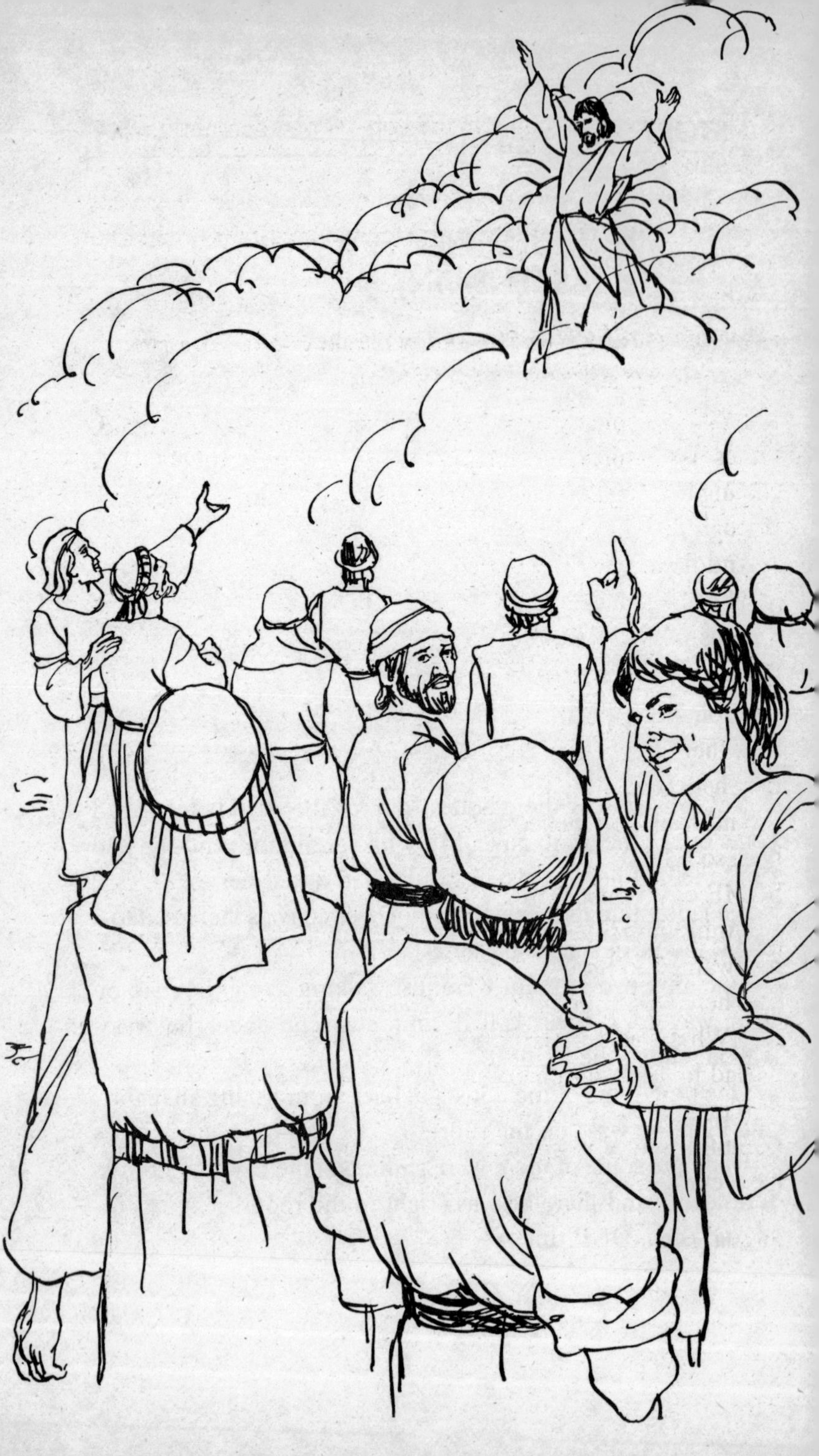

They were with him on the top of a mountain*—when suddenly—

Jesus began to rise up into the air, right before their very eyes! Up—up—UP—until a big cloud covered him up and he was GONE!

Why they just stood there staring at the sky. They were absolutely SPEECHLESS. And while they were staring—

Two angels suddenly stood right alongside them!

"Why are you staring up into heaven?" the two angels said. "Jesus is coming back again. Don't you remember? He's coming back again exactly the same way you just saw him go—through the clouds!"

And then they DID remember.

Of course!

Jesus had told them—a long, LONG time ago that he was going away. And they had been so sad.

"Going away?" they had said. "Going AWAY? OH NO!" And then they had all talked at once. "We will go with you," they had said.

And Jesus had looked at their sad faces, and oh, his eyes had been so KIND. "You cannot go with me NOW," he said. "But SOME day, you can."

"Ahhhhh—SOME day," they had thought. And then they had wanted to know—

Where was he going?

What was it LIKE?

And he had told them:

"I'm going to get a new home ready for you. It will be more beautiful than this world. More beautiful than anything you have ever SEEN. Or than anything you could even IMAG-

---

* Mount of Olives.

INE." And he had gone on to tell them about heaven, where no one will ever be sick and no one will every cry and no one will ever be unhappy. "And some day you can come and live there with me forever," he had said.

Of course!

They remembered, they remembered—

They couldn't be with him NOW. But SOME DAY—

They remembered, they remembered—

And they ran and ran to tell all the people!

LET'S TALK ABOUT THE BIBLE STORY

Everything in the Bible is according to God's plan. He made the world, and it was JUST RIGHT. He planned for Jesus to be born, and he WAS. He planned for Jesus to die for us, and he DID. He planned for Jesus to rise again, and he DID. He planned for Jesus to go back to heaven and prepare a place for us, and he DID. And he plans for Jesus to come again, and he WILL! Isn't that all good news?

A BIBLE VERSE TO LEARN

Jesus said, "*I will come and get you, so that you can always be with me where I am.*" (John 14:3, *TLB*)

LET'S TALK TO GOD

Dear God, we thank you that we can be with you some day in heaven. Help us to love you and tell others about you while we're waiting. In Jesus' name, Amen.

NOW FIND THIS STORY IN YOUR BIBLE

It's in Mark 16:12-20 and Luke 24:13-53 and Acts 1:1-12.

Jesus Loves Me, Jesus Loves Me

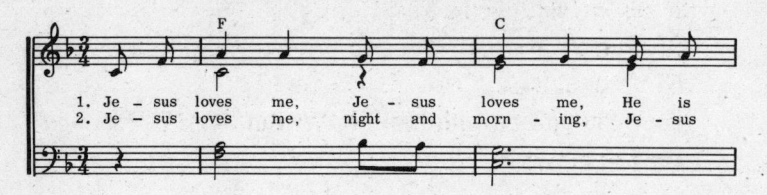

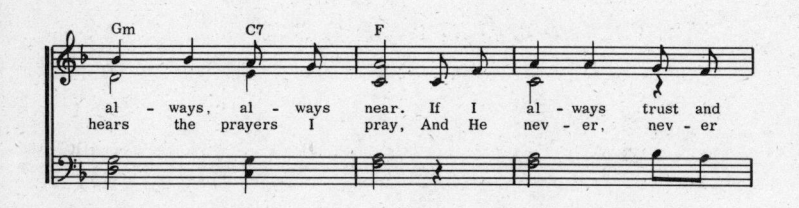

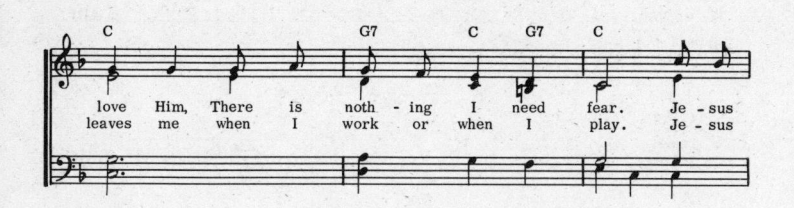

1. Jesus loves me, Jesus loves me, He is always, always near. If I always trust and love Him, There is nothing I need fear. Jesus loves me, Jesus loves me. He is always, always near.
2. Jesus loves me, night and morning, Jesus hears the prayers I pray, And He never, never leaves me when I work or when I play. Jesus loves me, night and morning, Jesus hears the prayers I pray.

Words and Music: Traditional.